How Does Disney Do That?

Praise for How Does Disney Do That?

"James Warda invites us to board the emotional roller coaster of Disney's enchanting universe, where every ride, every detail, is a testament to the power of imagination. With anecdotes that blend humor and sincerity, he peels back the layers of wonder and invites us to ask, 'How does Disney do that?' Strap in, hold tight, and prepare for a journey that will touch your heart and reignite your sense of awe."

—*David A. Bossert, former producer and creative director, Walt Disney Animation Studios, and author of* The House of the Future *and* The Nightmare Before Christmas Visual Companion

"*How Does Disney Do That?* is an essential read for anyone captivated by the magic and wonder of Disney, and who wants to peek behind the curtain to further deepen their appreciation for the timeless enchantment Disney offers...a must-have for any Disney fan's collection."

—*Lou Mongello, speaker, mentor, author, and host of* WDW Radio Disney Podcast

"*How Does Disney Do That?* is written with sincere warmth and no small amount of wit. It promises to enrich the experience of visiting a park for Disney fans and provide professionals from any sector with a solid grounding in the emotional and philosophical aspects of storytelling. It's an uplifting read for students considering a creative career or emerging professionals in the field."

—*Blooloop.com*

"These are my people! How do we so naturally become a part of the story? From casual guests turned absolute addicts to entertainment pros...he astutely interviews a massive collection of 'Disney people' who form an intangible, unshakable, and intensely personal bond with one of the world's biggest brands in search of the answer."

—*Stephanie Shuster, CEO & owner,* WDW Magazine

Story quotes

"You have to be emotionally sincere (when designing experiences). Emotions override our intellect...to create valid emotion, you have to have valid emotions. You have to feel them yourself, and then you have to be able to say, 'How could other people feel them based on what I intend to do?'"

—*Joe Rohde, former Disney Imagineer and Disney Legend, recipient of the TEA Lifetime Achievement Award, and Explorer's Club member*

"It's that commitment to story that brings a lump to our throats and a tear to our eyes when we go on Disney attractions and see Disney movies, because Walt's original concept is coming through in that moment to the guests and audience. And it happens generation after generation. I was a small part of Disney, but I'm so proud of having been connected with a genius."

—*Willie Ito, legendary animator for Disney, Warner Bros. Cartoons, and Hanna-Barbera Productions*

"When I was twelve, I remember standing on Main Street in Disneyland as it got dark. The lights started coming on along all those gingerbread buildings, a horse car was clopping quietly by, I could hear the whistle of the steam train, and suddenly it was twilight on a tranquil American small city street in 1908. And I thought, 'I want to stay here forever.' And, in a way, I did."

—*Richard Snow, author of* Disney's Land: Walt Disney and the Invention of the Amusement Park That Changed the World, *former editor-in-chief of American Heritage magazine, consultant for* Glory *and other motion pictures, and writer for PBS on the Burns brothers'* Civil War *and Rick Burns'* Coney Island

"We started with story. And, though many guests won't notice all the details...they can feel them."

—*Dan Cockerell, former VP of EPCOT, Disney's Hollywood Studios, and Magic Kingdom parks; author and consultant*

How
Does
Disney
Do
That?

How Disney Makes Us *Feel*
And Why It Matters

James Warda

RIVERSHORE
PRESS

For Gina.

None of this would have happened without you.

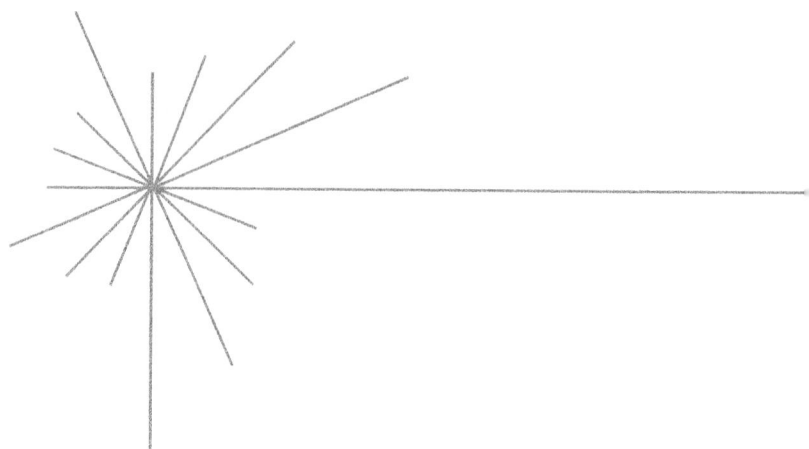

Contents

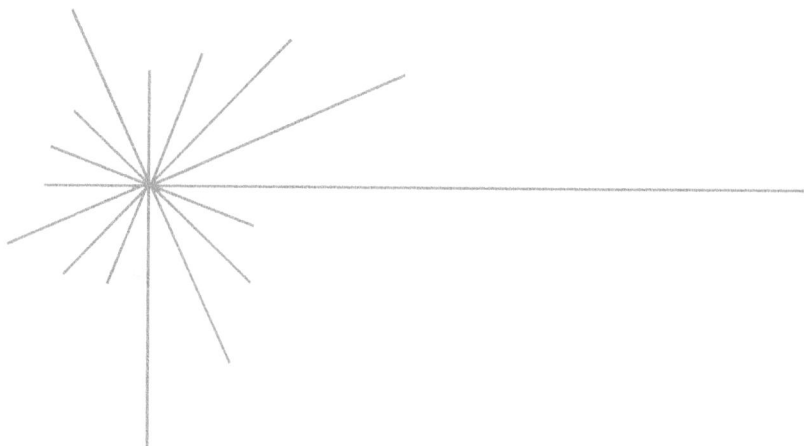

I spent my career as an Imagineer, working in an industry commonly referred to as "themed entertainment." Through most of that career I have been convinced, and have insisted to others, that this work is important and worthy of thoughtful consideration.

The word *entertainment* itself is worthy of consideration. It's commonly used to suggest something trivial, like amusement. But that is not what the word *entertain* means. The word *entertain* is related to words like *retain* and *contain*. If to retain is to hold something back, and to contain is to hold something within, then to entertain is to hold something between. To be entertained is to be suspended in the middle of something, to be held somewhere, immersed.

To be truly entertained, then, is a rare and wonderful thing. My erstwhile colleagues at Walt Disney Imagineering, and their operating partners throughout Disney Parks and Resorts, are some of the world's best at creating this transformative state of actual entertainment. Because such entertainment is rare, it excites curiosity as to why this is so and how this can be done.

Foreword

It's like watching a magician's sleight of hand trick. We want to stay in the magic of the moment but we must admit that we wonder "How is that done?" James Warda's book and its explorations are the byproduct of such curiosity.

These entertainments are created for you, and you have no obligation to do anything more than let yourself be suspended, to sit back and enjoy the show, no questions asked. But for those who are interested in how and why things work, it will be worth your while to follow the thoughts of someone who has looked for the answers.

Joe Rohde
Santa Barbara, California
December 2023

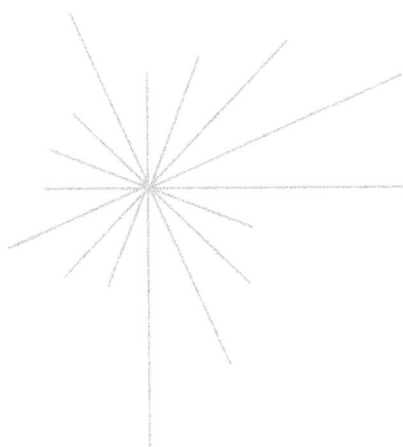

Introduction

"The most important aim of any of the fine arts is to get a purely emotional response from the beholder."

Walt Disney

To paraphrase Walt Disney, it all started with a mouse.

For me, it was a banshee.

You see, I cried while sitting on a "banshee" on the *Flight of Passage* attraction at Walt Disney World. Well, "cried" might be too strong a word. More like a tear or two brimming in my eyes. But I won't haggle, so let's just go with "cried."

Ok, now back to the banshee.

A "banshee," or "mountain banshee" to be exact, is a fictional creation that looks like a cross between a dragon and pterodactyl. With an adult wingspan of over 40 feet, it was ridden by Na'vi hunters, inhabitants of the fictional planet Pandora in James Cameron's 2009 movie, *Avatar*.

Disney opened a new land, Pandora—The World of Avatar, a highly detailed reproduction of the planet, in its Animal Kingdom Park in 2017. Former Imagineer and Disney Legend Joe Rohde led the creative efforts on the design of the new world, including the *Flight of Passage* attraction. Rohde was also the lead designer for the entire Animal Kingdom Park.

Because humans can't survive in Pandora's atmosphere, Earth scientists combine human and Na'vi DNA to create Na'vi clones. Humans then remotely pilot these clones, which are called "avatars."

It all began with a banshee

In 2021 my wife, Gina, and I decided to visit our son Matthew in Orlando. Once he heard we were coming, he excitedly started telling me about two new attractions I needed to ride at Disney. The first one, *Rise of the Resistance*, had opened in 2019 in the Galaxy's Edge *Star Wars*-themed world at Disney's Hollywood Studios Park. The second was *Flight of Passage* at Animal Kingdom Park; it had opened a bit earlier in 2017. Gina had already ridden *Flight of Passage* with Matthew.

As he would normally do with new attractions, and as a huge theme park enthusiast ever since he was, well, a toddler, my son made me promise I wouldn't look at any preview videos or even read about *Flight of Passage*. The same restriction applied to both Gina and me for *Rise*. He wanted us to fully experience our "first time" with him.

We loved that.

After arriving, we all rode *Rise of the Resistance*. It was as exciting as advertised and more of an "experience" than an attraction, putting you in the role of a *Star Wars* rebel being captured by the First Order. Other than the ride itself, though, what made it really stand out is that, unlike other attractions and venues at Disney World, the Cast Members were supposed to be *mean*.

"Mean?" you ask, with one eyebrow raised Spock-like. Yep, mean! Now, of course "Disney mean" is still pretty nice, and they were, after all, just acting, but it added a fun bit of spice to the experience.

While gathering Matthew Krul's story for this book (Matthew is the owner of the wonderful *Imagination Skyway* Disney podcast and community), he mentioned the possibility of pledging allegiance to the First Order on *Rise of the Resistance*.

So, the next time I went on, I tried it. Of course, there were two benefits to doing so. One, I might be able to get special treatment for "selling out" and two, I would for sure get eye rolls from my wife and son. As soon as we were ushered out of our captured ship, I slyly whispered to one of the First Order "guards" that I wanted to pledge allegiance to them. After smirking, he responded, "Well, we captured you WITH the rebels, so you obviously already CHOSE. Now move along." Clearly I need to rethink my whole approach to rebellion and might need to recycle my "I ♥ the First Order" button.

The next day, after escaping the faintly evil clutches of the "sweetly mean" First Order, we went to Animal Kingdom Park and its *Flight of Passage*. And there, on that day, this book and the entire *How Does Disney Do That?* project was born.

Now to be honest, before going on the attraction, I must admit I didn't have a strong emotional connection to *Avatar*. I had seen the original movie and was impressed by its special effects, but that was about the extent of it. So I wasn't going in with huge expectations or a significant attachment.

Which is very important, and something I'll touch on later. This aspect made it different from *Rise of the Resistance*, where I went in, like so many others did, with the *Star Wars* saga having been such a big part of my life (and, yes, I'm old enough to remember when the first one came out in theaters and was simply called *Star Wars*).

It all started while waiting in one of the most elaborate Disney queues I had ever seen. From a slow climb through the "Valley of Mo'ara" outside, surrounded by exotic trees and plants and the sounds of birds and waterfalls, we entered a winding path inside a mountain, passing by walls covered with cave paintings. Soon the path took us through a dark jungle filled with bioluminescent flowers and trees before heading into an extensive human laboratory filled with Pandoran specimens and textbooks, including a very impressive full-size floating avatar—all leading to the flight chamber and "banshees."

Yes, the details of the queue did what many Disney queues do best—it made me forget I was in one. And invited me into a story.

> The queue sequence on *Flight of Passage* can vary for a number of reasons, such as how long the waits are, and can also include several pre-show stops along the way.

Next, we were "linked" to our avatars and proceeded to the flight chamber. My son and I walked to our assigned "banshees," two ride vehicles situated next to each other that, to me, resembled futuristic Jet Skis. They were arranged in a line along with fourteen others, all facing a long, metallic wall with what appeared to be closed shutters. The darkened room was also made more mysterious by accents of muted color-shifting lighting and a machine-like pulsing sound from behind the walls.

After climbing on and putting on our 3-D goggles, the back-pieces on the machines rotated up and locked us firmly, but comfortably, in place. With my anticipation building (ok, yes, and just a tinge of anxiety, the evil twin of anticipation), we looked down at digital readouts in front of us as our avatars "connected neural networks" with our banshees.

> According to *Avatar* legend, bonding with a mountain banshee is a critical step and important rite of passage in the life of a Na'vi hunter. A Na'vi hunter, including avatars, can connect to a banshee through a neural interface that allows animal and rider to move together seamlessly.

At that point, I glanced over to see how Matthew was doing. As I expected, he looked calm but excited. I didn't expect any less since he had ridden the attraction many times already, plus he never seems to get nervous on rides, even the biggest and tallest. Whereas, I *was* getting nervous, as evidenced by the fact that my eyes kept darting back to those still-closed shutters.

Now, of course, I *knew* I was at Disney World, and I *knew* I was safe, but getting unnerved by the unknown is just part of the human condition. Plus, it's an important feature of many Disney stories and attractions, helping to build necessary tension that later releases into laughter, "Happily Ever Afters," and probably a marriage and carriage.

Finally, though, it was time...and the shutters slid up.

As soon as they did, we literally dropped into the skies of Pandora, sweeping down into a world that stretched out to what seemed like 360 degrees all around us, horizon to horizon. The scents and sights and sounds of forests and flowers, the vibrant colors of the clouds, and the ocean's surf crashing against the sand at the same time as our faces were slightly misted. And this all happening while we were accompanied by a seemingly endless variety of Pandoran animals and birds, our fellow Na'vi hunters riding their own banshees, stately floating mountains, and of course, predators—a necessary ingredient in any rite, or flight, of passage worth its salt. Like villains in a Disney movie.

Yes, the attraction had already touched on all of the five senses. And it was about to touch on the sixth.

Unlike the 1999 Bruce Willis film, *The Sixth Sense*, the sixth sense I refer to here is an "intuitive" sense that some people believe goes beyond the most commonly known five senses of sight, hearing, touch, smell, and taste. Something that transcends. More on that later.

As I flew on my banshee, hearing and feeling it "breathing" beneath me while it dove and swerved, with its "lungs" inflating and deflating against my legs, I looked around again. But this time, for some reason, I did so more calmly, getting used to the movement.

In short, I paid attention.

And it was at that moment, as I was taking it all in, that my eyes brimmed with tears.

Wait, what?

Tears?!

Yes, tears.

And as soon as I noticed them, I realized how embarrassed I was, and to be honest, a bit surprised. After all, there I was, 57 years old at the time, knowing I was at Disney World. Knowing I was on a ride. With my adult son. And, beneath the surface, knowing I didn't even have an emotional connection to the story of Pandora—and yet I was getting emotional!

So, why was I tearing up? What exactly was going on, and what would my son think if he happened to glance over?

Of course, after the fact, when I was thinking more clearly and was not so overwhelmed by what I was feeling, I realized there would have been no way my son could have seen those few tears beneath my goggles, especially while we were both still "flying" in a darkened room. But in the moment, as it was happening, the only thing I was thinking about was whether I'd be able to squeeze a finger between my cheek and goggles to wipe the tears away.

And then something changed. Still not sure how to describe it.

Like in Dr. Seuss' *How the Grinch Stole Christmas*. You know the scene, when the Grinch hears the Whoville citizens singing on Christmas morning, even though so much had been taken from them. "It started in low. Then it started to grow."

As did my realization of why I was crying. The name of the emotion that had brought forth those tears.

Wonder.

Yep, *that* wonder. The one Merriam-Webster defines as "rapt attention or astonishment at something awesomely mysterious or new to one's experience."

Of course, now, looking back, I would respectfully add two more words to that definition, right before "mysterious." They'd be "magical and..."

Yes, that's exactly how it felt right then. Magical *and* mysterious.

It was the type of wonder that children often feel, like it's just another part of their day. Like when they're outside and they get down on their hands and knees, dirt be darned, to check out an ant. For them that ant is fascinating, especially when it carries a leaf many times its size and weight. Or laughing in amazement while catching snowflakes on their tongues. Wait, something from the sky that is beautiful *and* ok to eat, too? Wow, who knew?!

Fascination. Amazement.

Just other words for "wonder."

But here's the thing...when do we, as adults, get to feel wonder? Of being able to suspend our built-up-through-the-years-of-practice disbelief enough to allow the illusion to become reality, to not try to figure out what's behind the curtain, at least for a moment? And even, in those more perfect moments, to forget that there's even a curtain there. Where does wonder slip in between going to work and paying the bills and fixing the gutters and trying to figure out what to make for dinner while the laundry calls and the dog scratches at the back door to be walked?

Of course, I'm not including those "wondrous milestone moments" many of us do get to experience, like getting married and having children and grandchildren. Or when we realize we've fallen in love, finally begun living our purpose, or come through a dark and difficult time, stronger and wiser.

For example, my personal milestones include feeling a sense of wonder when I first saw Gina, my soon-to-be-wife, at the back of the church, equal parts beauty and grace. When I did, I remember quickly inhaling air with a "Whoosh!" Translation? "Wow, she's amazing!"

I have also often felt wonder for many reasons with my children, Jeremy, Matthew, and Alexandra, as they've grown up. Usually, though, it came back to two things—their kindness and courage. And with each moment, again like the Grinch, my heart grew three sizes, but really oh so much bigger. Then later, as my wife and I held our first grandchild. One who literally can turn us into puddles with a simple smile.

Yes, I had definitely felt wonder before.

But not like this, on a seemingly normal day.

And definitely not on a *park attraction*!

After the ride ended I took off my goggles, stood up, and while still a little off-balance from what I'd felt, excitedly told Matthew how incredible it had been. Then, as we walked out into the daylight, my mind instantly cleared.

And at that specific moment, one frozen in time, I silently asked myself, "How does Disney *do* that?"

> *(Insert powerful John Williams-like symphonic build, rising to a cymbal crash, to mark the significance of the moment.)*

Now, when I asked myself that question, I also instinctively knew I wasn't necessarily asking about the technical "how" and "what" behind how Disney had just made me feel. Like how they designed the ride vehicles, what they used to create the different sounds and smells, how the screen worked, and so on. Although, that kind of "behind-the-scenes" information is actually compelling to me, as it is to many Disney fans. And you will find a good amount of that in this book.

No, I knew I was asking about something less tangible, something behind and beyond the five senses. Something I couldn't quite put into words and still honestly struggle with.

Which is why I decided to write about it.

My message in a bottle came back

"Huh?" I can hear you saying. "You couldn't put it into words, so you wanted to write about it? How does *that* work?"

Well, to tell you the truth, I believe that many writers figure out what they want to write about by...wait for it...*writing about it*. I definitely fall into that category. To find out what I want to say, the way I want to say it, and what I believe it ultimately means, I often have to start writing first. And let me tell you, writing a sentence like this one and not knowing where it's going to go and how it's going to end may not be considered courageous by many, but that white space just ahead of the cursor sure can make me pause from time to time and take a settling breath, before checking that my hands, arms, legs, and feet are all inside the vehicle, and then start moving forward again.

So, why *did* I want to write about it?

Because at that moment, having just come from the attraction, with the question "How does Disney do that?" still circling in the air above my head, and that feeling of wonder still humming inside my brain, I knew I had seen and felt something special. Something, as I said earlier, beyond the five senses. That old sixth sense creeping in.

Knowing that, I realized there were people on the *other* end of that experience who might have felt something similar. Those who created the attraction that had just "facilitated" my feeling of wonder, those who planned, designed, and built the attraction and its story, the Cast Members who made it come to life and keep it maintained, and everyone in between.

And, really, that's the main hypothesis of this book. That for me to feel wonder, the people who created the experience must have felt it first and wanted to pass it on. A hypothesis that would soon prove itself true when I heard former Imagineer and Disney Legend Joe Rohde, responsible for the very attraction that started this whole thing, confirm it.

I was watching an episode of Zeitgeist Design and Production's *Spirit of the Time* Zoomcast, and there was Joe Rohde explaining why emotions are so important to the design of an attraction:

> "You have to be emotionally sincere. Emotions override our intellect. People think too much. Much as I am a thinking person, in the end, the things we do ride on emotion, and in order to create valid emotion, you have to have valid emotions. You have to feel them yourself, and then you have to be able to say, 'How can I help other people feel them based on what I intend to do?' Emotional sincerity will save almost anything."
>
> *Shared here with his approval.*

So with all of that still pinballing in my head, I made the decision to first write about the experience in my *Where Are We Going So Fast?* blog for the Chicago Tribune Media Group. Named after my first book, *Where Are We Going So Fast?: Finding the Sacred in Everyday Moments*, this platform now gave me the opportunity to share my story with a large group of readers. I wanted to find out if others felt the same. Why? So that I could hopefully begin to figure out what had happened, whether anybody else had a similar reaction, and ultimately what it meant—because as they say, *mystery loves company* (sorry, couldn't help it). But if you don't think I was a little anxious admitting what had happened to me, well, please, oh please, thinketh again.

So I published it. And I didn't have to wait long; I soon received over a hundred responses back, from men and women alike, saying they, too, had cried on *Flight of Passage* and other Disney attractions. I wrote a second article, describing what people had shared (the true joy of a columnist—when one article turns into two!).

Then, to add to the growing amount of evidence that "something was going on here," a few weeks later I was watching *The Imagineering Story* by documentarian Leslie Iwerks on Disney+. I saw Imagineers on the series also getting emotional as *they* talked about the attractions they worked on. (Since then, I've also had the privilege of talking to many individuals with an Imagineering background and saw for myself as the emotion came up.)

Leslie Iwerks is many things: an Academy Award® and Emmy®-nominated director and producer, including director of *The Imagineering Story* on Disney+; author of *The Imagineering Story: The Official Biography of Walt Disney Imagineering*; CEO and creative director of Iwerks & Co.; daughter of legendary Disney animator, Don Iwerks; and granddaughter of Ub Iwerks, one of Walt Disney's original business partners, special effects innovators, and animators, who, according to the Disney D23 website, is "credited with sketching Mickey Mouse for the first time."

To complete the chain of coincidences linking together in front of me, I happened to connect with former Imagineering creative executive and founder of The Designer's Creative Studio, Theron Skees, through a LinkedIn post from The Disney Institute. Theron listened to my "How does Disney do that?" question and immediately let me know that, as an Imagineer, he was always looking to ask guests an important question about the attractions he worked on—"How did it make you *feel*?" (Since that meeting, Theron has become my business partner and main contributor to this book, providing "Theron's Keys" throughout. Oh, yes, and he's a heck of a guy.)

Theron Skees, former Walt Disney Imagineering (WDI) creative executive with over 23 years of experience and founder of The Designer's Creative Studio, shared the following:

"For me, it all started when James connected with me asking the question, "How does Disney do that?" about the wonder he felt on *Flight of Passage*. His question struck me because it was the flipside of the question I had asked myself as an Imagineer for so many years and continue to ask. Namely, 'How will people feel after going on this attraction I helped create—and will it be what I hoped they would feel?'

"I never felt more excited, more in touch with the individuals that I created those experiences for, than when I actually got to meet them. Because the guest is who I'm thinking about the whole time I'm committing this passion, this excitement, this expertise, all the late nights learning about how to do new things, to blow your mind, to make your life special and create an experience that locks in your memory. It could be through tears, through gasps of excitement. It could be, you know, you grabbing your loved one's hand tighter in that moment, and it could be forming memories that last a lifetime.

"So, I loved the idea that, with his question, James metaphorically knocked on the door of those who create the attractions and other elements and gave us a chance to provide an answer for him, and for all fans that will read this book.

"The ones who say, 'Please explain all this to me. I'm a guest looking in. Help me understand why I feel this way.' And we answer, 'Hi Mr. or Mrs. Guest, I'm Mr. or Mrs. Imagineer and I'd be glad to share this with you because I've been thinking about you the entire time I've been creating all of this."

Yes, it turns out that an Imagineer's ultimate measure of success includes whether they helped guests *feel* something. And ideally the feeling the Imagineer hoped they would.

So, with all that, why are we here? Why did I write this book, who did I write it for, how is it unique, how is it structured, and how will readers be able to keep the conversation going long after they've finished the last page?

Well, whew...let's take those one at a time.

Why this book?

I wrote this book, and collected its stories, because that day on *Flight of Passage* I saw and felt something important that I wanted to share with you in hopes that you've felt it, too, at some point in your life. Or will. So that we can talk about it and figure out together what it means. And so that people from both sides, fans and those who create the experiences, can "compare emotional notes."

Because I believe that this all means something very important.

Something just beyond that screen all around me on *Flight of Passage*, but still before my eyes. Something connecting me to all Disney fans who had ever felt, were feeling, or would feel that way, that sense of wonder or other powerful feeling. That connected all of us to something we loved.

And why, in fact, we do that. Not only label ourselves "Disney fans," but also live in such a way that even the local Barnes & Noble knows to call us when the latest Disney book hits the shelves. Why *are* we so *passionate* about a global multimedia conglomerate?! How can Disney possibly cause us to feel the magic of escape and reassurance, and that there are really such things as a "second star to the right"?

At the end of J.M. Barrie's book, *Peter Pan* (upon which Disney's movie is based), Peter says, "There it is, Wendy! Second star to the right and straight on 'til morning." As a side note, the quote was famously used again at the end of *Star Trek VI: The Undiscovered Country*, when Ensign Pavel Chekov asks Captain James T. Kirk what he should set as the next destination for their starship, the *Enterprise*. Captain Kirk replies with the quote. And, yes, I'm a nerd.

Well, I believe it's because, in addition to a mouse (and a banshee), it all started with a very basic, very human longing from a not-so-basic, but oh-so-human man who somehow turned a longing into *be*-longing.

Now, I know that's not news. We all can recall the stories of how Walt Disney grew up hard under a harder father, and then went from rags to riches to rags and back again several times, all while turning the entertainment world...ah, scratch that, I mean the *whole* world, on its ear. Two large round ones, in fact.

Along the way, of course, the list of innovations that Walt and his team created would most definitely have needed the "print both sides of the page" function on your printer, or you'd run out of paper quickly.

Synchronize sound to a cartoon? Check.

Build a camera that turns one-dimensional animation into multi-dimensional images the camera can "move" through, which means you can, too? Check.

Create a full-length animated feature film with complex characters that makes the audience not just laugh, but also cry—something many didn't think was possible? Check.

Realize the full power of merchandising when tied to beloved characters like Mickey Mouse and Davey Crockett? Oh, and create a group for Mickey Mouse fans that was the original "Cool Club"? Check.

Build a theme park for families at a time when amusement parks didn't exactly bring to mind images of cleanliness and virtue? And do it within a year! Check.

Fund that theme park primarily by partnering with a struggling-at-the-time television network on a new show named *after* the theme park that also acted as a commercial for it? Check.

Create audio-animatronic figures that, year by year, have gotten more and more life-like, to the point that I just had to check in the mirror to make sure I'm not one? Check.

And the list, like the beat, goes on.

One man. One vision. One relentless mindset to persist and innovate. All fueled by one longing. A longing, I believe, for something that he didn't have as a child and wanted desperately as an adult, for him and his own children. And, in the process, for all of us.

And that longing lives to this day and comes—despite the twists and turns expected whenever you get a large group of people together to run an organization—from a company committed to keeping Walt's vision alive. To create that magic for children as they grow and, once they're adults, turn them back into children again.

Like Walt and his company did, years later, for me on *Flight of Passage*. Reminding me of how I used to feel as a young boy watching *The Wonderful World of Disney* on TV.

Wonder Full, indeed.

So, really, that wonder I felt was wonder Walt and his company wanted—and still want—all their fans to feel.

Which says we matter to them. Yes, we may often have to pay to feel that way, but that doesn't mean it's the only reason they do it. And I can tell you that with confidence after talking with so many former Disney executives, Imagineers, Cast Members, and others. I heard it in their words and saw it in their eyes.

We matter to them.

Which is also why I decided to write this book. Not only to figure out the answer to my question after getting off *Flight of Passage* that day, but because Disney makes us feel like we matter. And in a world that so often feels like it's dedicated to doing the exact opposite, *that* matters.

After meeting Theron, we also agreed that I would write this book in a way that would share stories from both sides of the attraction—from guests as well as from those who created the experiences for them—in a way that mirrored the conversation he and I were already having. Because that's what we, as humans, do. Converse. Share our stories. It's how we connect what's inside to the outside.

Most importantly, I hope that, as you read this book, you'll remember your own stories about how Disney makes you feel and also find new ones to tell. And how, by sharing our stories, we remember just how small the world really is... international dolls and catchy song included.

If there's one thing I've learned from being a Disney fan, it's how small a world it really is. A lesson I've learned over and over again, but most distinctly remember learning while standing in line with my wife and kids, who were young at the time, waiting to go on the *Dumbo* ride at the Magic Kingdom.

As we waited, our boys were bickering, exhausted from a long day in Florida's August sun (yes, we went in August, and no, being from the Midwest, we didn't fully appreciate what that actually meant before we arrived). Thankful for the momentary shade of the covered queue, I looked around at the families in line with us, seemingly from all different parts of the world, dealing with their own bickering kids, trying to pull them apart or otherwise distract them.

And at that moment, I realized again just how similar we all are. That, no matter where we live, we often deal with the same things. A realization made possible by Disney that day.

Who is this book for?

When I thought about who would read this book, three main audiences came to mind:

Disney fans who love everything Disney so much that every third photo at home is from a Disney park and every fifth kitchen towel is covered in those famous ears. For them, I hope the stories will bring the joy that comes from finding others who share their passion, hearing from those who create the experiences for them, and finding that they do, in fact, belong to something bigger.

Themed entertainment design professionals and students, and all those who work with them, at theme and amusement parks, on cruises, in convention centers, theaters, museums, and more, who want to create something that is felt and remembered. Yes, I hope the book will help them see the impact of what they do. And to always keep top-of-mind and tip-of-tongue the question for those they create experiences for: "How did it make you *feel?*"

Leaders, professionals, teams, and others, from all fields, profit and nonprofit alike, who can see the impact and importance of an organization like Disney creating such an enduring emotional connection with their fans. I hope they read this book and say, "Wow, how can we make our customers and clients love our organization enough to write a similar book about *us*?"

What makes this book unique?

First, *How Does Disney Do That?* focuses on the intangibles that go into creating experiences that make people feel—the "why's" such as emotion, passion, and commitment. Of course, along the way those who create the experiences will also share their more tangible takeaways, including the "what's" and "how's," such as planning, design, and production.

Second, many of the stories you'll find here came from our two online groups on Facebook and LinkedIn. Once you finish this book (or actually, right now would be a good time, too!), you can join these groups to be part of the ongoing conversation. We also have an Instagram page because, well, since a picture's worth a thousand words, and I typically have a lot to say, that works out well. Just search for "How Does Disney Do That?" on all these platforms. (Of course, over time we may find even more ways to stay connected.)

Third, the book includes stories from Give Kids The World Village® leaders and staff, and a portion of the book's proceeds will be donated to the Village.

The Give Kids The World Village® program in Kissimmee, Florida, is a nonprofit charity founded in partnership with the Walt Disney World® (WDW) Resort, in which critically ill children and their families visit the WDW parks and other Orlando theme parks and locations. The Village was founded by Henri Landwirth, a Holocaust survivor, Korean war veteran, hotelier, and friend of the original NASA Mercury astronauts, Walter Cronkite, and many others.

After vowing that every critically ill child who wished to visit Central Florida would have a place to stay, he founded the Village in partnership with organizations that included Walt Disney World, Universal Orlando Resort, Sea World Parks & Resorts Orlando, and Perkins Restaurant & Bakery. Many other companies and organizations also support them.

I was introduced to the group by Brian Collins, a former Imagineer you'll hear from later in this book. Thanks, Brian.

If you'd like to donate to this so-much-more-than-worthy organization that's also connected closely to Disney, visit our website at howdoesdisneydothat.com/charity. And thank you.

How is the book structured?

As with Disney, everything here starts with story. So, just as I did with this Introduction, I'll start most of the chapters with a personal story about how Disney makes me feel, and then share stories I've been honored to hear from Disney fans, those who created the experiences, and others. Then, at the end of most chapters you'll find several questions to bring out your Disney stories. You'll also find "Theron's Keys" throughout the book, where Theron Skees, my main contributor, shares his own stories and insights from over 23 years with Walt Disney Imagineering.

The chapters will focus on key themes that answer our main question: "How does Disney do that?" Themes that include the following:

- The power of storytelling
- Our human needs that need these stories
- How suspension of disbelief allows for the beginning of real belief
- Why Disney's "Welcome home" is more than just words
- How every detail matters at Disney—including the most "random" ones

How can we keep the conversation going after you finish the book?

Did you ever see "The End" on a Disney movie and wished it wouldn't? Sequels help with this. But what if you didn't have to leave the story at all?

Well, here, you don't.

Why? Because, as mentioned above, we created two *How Does Disney Do That?* groups—on Facebook and LinkedIn—

where, right now, Disney fans from all over the world are sharing their stories about how Disney makes them feel, while those who have a Disney Imagineering, leadership, or Cast Member background, are sharing their stories of what drove them to create these experiences. They're also joined there by voices of Disney-related authors, podcasters, magazine publishers, social group owners, influencers, and more. Plus, I'm interacting in the groups regularly—as are many of my contributors—so we can stay in touch that way.

So, come join the fun and share your story (again, just search for "How Does Disney Do That?" on either platform).

We'll be all ears.

But wait, there's more! You can also submit your stories at www.howdoesdisneydothat.com. I plan to continue gathering stories for future books in the *How Does Disney Do That?* series, so I'd love to hear what you have to share.

Once upon a time...

To inspire his team of artists and writers to create his studio's first full-length animated feature, Walt Disney gathered them all together one night in the original Disney Studios soundstage in Los Angeles. He proceeded to bring his vision for the 1937 film, *Snow White and the Seven Dwarfs*, to life for them, enthusiastically acting out all the parts and transforming himself into the characters, complete with distinct voices. The rest is history. Literally.

And it all started with *HIM* telling them a story.
And it all started with him telling them a *STORY*.

Wait, isn't this just saying the same thing twice? Hardly. I emphasized "him" the first time because I believe that for a story to truly have the power to transform us, we must believe in the storyteller.

Did Walt's employees believe in him? Well, I'll leave that to Disney historians. But, if you ask me my gut feeling, I'd say they did, even though he could be one of the most demanding people in the world, but with a way of making them feel part of something important. (More on believing in, and actually loving, the storyteller in Chapter One.)

I focused on "story" the second time because story is the vehicle of choice, the means of travel. It invites us in and carries us along, and in the end, changes us. When it's there, we know it. When it's not, the same. And either way, before we know it, we can typically feel it in the bones before it ever reaches the brain. (More on the power of Disney storytelling in Chapter Two.)

According to D23.com, *Snow White and the Seven Dwarfs* received a special Academy Award in 1939 consisting of one full-size Oscar and seven small Oscars, presented to Walt Disney by Shirley Temple. The film became the highest-grossing motion picture of all time, until surpassed by *Gone With the Wind*.

So, what *did* Walt do that evening? How did he inspire his team to do something that had never been done before and, in the process, change not only the art of animation but the arc of it? He did what great storytellers do with great stories: "animate" them. *Bring them to life.*

Which is why we're here. To share our stories, and in doing so, bring to life the feeling that we fans have for Disney, and Disney has for us. To show that there *is* magic behind the method. To know we are connected.

Because right now, in our world, I'm going to go out on a limb and say that we could all use a little more connection, a little more kindness, and a whole lot more magic.

Which is why I wrote this "love letter" to Disney (he said, unabashedly).

Because I firmly believe that, if Disney didn't exist, we'd need to create it.

James Warda
St. Cloud, Florida
December 2023

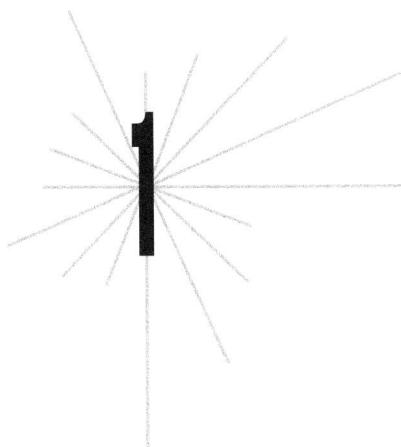

1 Falling in Love

"As he read, I fell in love the way you fall asleep: slowly, and then all at once."

The Fault in Our Stars by John Green

S o, there I was, a storyteller by trade, thinking this morning about what story to begin this chapter with...

...while sitting on the couch, eating cereal out of my bowl from the Disney "Home" line of merchandise, using my Mickey spoon from that same collection, while looking at the knickknacks on the shelf under our television where a small Mickey Mouse-shaped planter sits in front of one of our photo memory books from a trip to Disney World when the kids were young...

...and now, as I sit typing this chapter in my home office, surrounded by (in no particular order) my Disney World Annual Passholder magnets on the file cabinet to my left, and behind that cabinet, an early black and white photo of the Magic Kingdom construction site, with a superimposed image of Walt Disney walking in front of Cinderella Castle. And further away, down that same wall, a full-color framed Disney serigraph with Pinocchio pulling on Jiminy Cricket's coattails as Jiminy tries to storm off, while right behind me on a shelf is my son's *Golden Mickey* souvenir statue from our first Disney cruise (please don't ask me why my *son's* souvenir from that trip is in *my* office!), and another photo memory book from a Disney World trip with the kids.

Yes, as you can see, I'm a bit smitten, as are my wife and kids. So, what "smote" us? Disney's story? Of course. And, at the same time, the storyteller.

Disney itself.

Yep, I admit when I first saw the word "serigraph," I had to look it up. This is what I found at laasyaart.com: "A serigraph is a high quality, limited edition fine art print, made on high quality absorbent paper in collaboration between the artist and a professional printer."

My wife started my Disney story

As a kid, I liked Disney, but I didn't yet love it. At least that's how it feels looking back.

I do, of course, remember watching *The Wonderful World of Disney* on Sunday night TV back then. And going to Disney movies like *The Computer Wore Tennis Shoes* (Kurt Russell has had quite an interesting career). And, yes, I loved *Chitty Chitty Bang Bang*, which felt like a Disney movie to me as a kid. But, no, I didn't see the Disney classic animated films growing up (my mom instead took my brother and me to see the *Dr. Phibes* movies; please don't ask). I also never went to Disneyland or Disney World. And though I knew Mickey, I was more of a *Speed Racer* guy.

According to disneyplus.com, the 1969 film *The Computer Wore Tennis Shoes*, starring a young Kurt Russell, was about a "bumbling college student who is accidentally transformed from half-wit to genius in an electrifying computer mishap, though things go south when gangsters realize he knows the ins-and-outs of their gambling rings." And, no, I'm not making that up.

Though not officially a Disney movie, *Chitty Chitty Bang Bang* had a strong Disney influence. The music was written by Robert and Richard Sherman, who wrote many songs for Disney movies and attractions. Plus, it starred Dick Van Dyke, who had starred in *Mary Poppins* three years before. And it was choreographed by Marc Breaux, who had also choreographed *Mary Poppins*.

So, when *did* I fall in love with Disney?

Well, for that answer, I'll start with a quote from John Green's 2012 novel, *The Fault in Our Stars*, from the moment where a young woman realizes she has fallen for a young man: "As he read, I fell in love the way you fall asleep: slowly, and then all at once."

And I'm guessing you didn't expect to see a quote from *The Fault in Our Stars*, a story about two star-crossed, critically ill teenagers, in a Disney-related book. In a 2014 interview on reddit.com, when asked about the quote, John Green said it was inspired by a quote from Ernest Hemingway's novel, *The Sun Also Rises*, where a character is asked how he went bankrupt. "Two ways," he answers. "Gradually, then suddenly..."

What does that "gradually, then suddenly" look like in the real world? Well, allow me to illustrate.

After I got married, my wife—who *had* grown up loving the Disney classic animated films and visited Disney World in the 1970s as a kid—started planning Disney World trips for our family.

Now, when I say "planning," what I really mean is "strategically and comprehensively building Excel spreadsheets and activating her enhanced tactical planning experience, insider Disney knowledge, and differentiating expertise so that our mission to enjoy every moment of every minute of the Disney experience would be noted, documented, and filed for future reference."

In short, my wife is a planner.

Kicking off our adventures, we first visited Disney World as a family in August of 1998. And I know that being scorched to death in the white-hot center of Central Florida's summer, while wading through crowds and standing in long lines for rides, probably doesn't sound like the beginning of a love story. But, really, isn't that how every great love story starts in the movies? Two people are thrown together on an impossible mission. They're very different. There's no way they'll get along. They argue constantly. Yet, somehow, miraculously, somewhere along the way, as they each bend down to pick up a critical dossier from the desk, they lock eyes and...well, you know the rest.

In fact, that sounds like some Disney movies we know, too, right? Think *Mulan, Tangled, Aladdin, Frozen,* and *Beauty and the Beast,* just to name a few. And how, in each, something that wasn't there before, suddenly is. Or, if you will, they fell in love "slowly, and then all at once."

After that first trip, we didn't go back for four years.

Why?

Well, for many reasons, not including the Florida sun, most of which I'm sure you'd understand. Like the regular hurries and worries of life and dealing with a budget that just wouldn't budge. But, after that, like some magical multiplying mathematical progression, the trips to Disney World increased in frequency, and subsequently included Disneyland and Disney Cruises:

- 1998 (Disney World)
- 2002 (Disney World)
- 2004 (Disney World)
- 2007 (Disney World)
- 2008 (Disney World/Disney Cruise)
- 2009 (Disney World/Disney Cruise)
- 2010 (Disney World)
- 2011 (Disney World)
- 2012 (Disney World)
- 2013 (Disney World)
- 2014 (Disney World)
- 2015 (Disney World)
- 2016 (Disneyland)
- 2020 (Disney World)
- 2021 (Disney World)
- 2021: moved to Florida, about 30 miles from Disney World!

My wife's original Disney planning documents are now housed at the National Archives with the Constitution of the United States and the Declaration of Independence, which as you know, the Archives got back from Ben Gates after he "borrowed" it in Disney's *National Treasure.*

But, looking back at this series of dates now, I still ask myself, "When exactly did *it* happen?!" When did looking forward to seeing Disney World become *needing* to see it? When did our last days of a Disney vacation go from being simply sad to demanding that we immediately start planning our next trip on the plane ride home? In all, when did something fun and entertaining become more committed than that, to the point where we didn't just bring our family to Disney, but Disney became *part* of our family and followed us home?

Getting to the bottom, or top, of it

Well, as it is anytime we try to answer the question of when we fell in love with someone or something, I can't tell you the exact time or place we did with Disney. But I can tell you that it *did* happen. And that, for about twenty-five years now, we've been going strong, Disney and us. In fact, we've all updated our relationship statuses.

Now, of course, any great love story is part art and part science.

The art is the "magic," the stuff that happens that we can't explain but most definitely feel.

Then there's the science. Why technically would we fall in love with Disney? What does it do for us? And can I prove my second hypothesis that, if Disney didn't exist, we'd need to create it?

To understand the science part of it, let's first listen to Abraham. No, not Abraham Lincoln's animatronic at Disneyland, but Abraham Maslow, an American psychologist who created Maslow's Hierarchy of Needs, a model of how humans typically meet their needs in an ascending order.

I know, I know. First, I reference *The Fault in Our Stars*, and now I'm referencing Maslow's Hierarchy of Needs...in a book about Disney. Well, yeah, that's how I roll.

To paraphrase simplypsychology.org, the Hierarchy of Needs is "a motivational theory in which, moving upwards, the needs are biological and physiological (food, clothing), safety (job security), love and belonging (friendship, trust, love), esteem (for oneself, for acceptance), cognitive (knowledge, curiosity), aesthetic (appreciation, search for beauty), self-actualization (realizing personal potential), and transcendence (mystical experiences, aesthetic experiences)."

Typically, each level must be satisfied before the next one up is pursued. (And, for anyone who has gotten "hangry" and could think of nothing else until their hunger was satisfied or has been outside in subzero temperatures without a hat and gloves and could think of nothing else until they were back inside, they'll understand.)

Looking at the hierarchy below (I promise it's the only figure in the book), I believe Disney can fulfill *all* these needs. How? Well, for that answer, let's use the example of a typical day during a typical Disney World visit, like staying at the Beach Club Resort and going to EPCOT. As we do, let's see how many needs on Maslow's hierarchy we can check off:

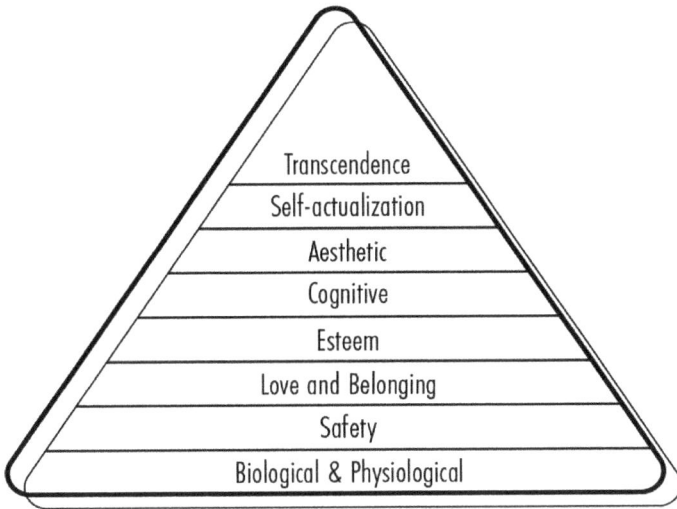

Maslow's Hierarchy of Needs Model

Biological and physiological (food, clothing, sleep): If you're at EPCOT or its surrounding resorts, finding food is *not* going to be a problem—it tends to appear every seven feet, including the awe-inspiring Kitchen Sink treat at the Beach Club Resort. And, as I understand it, you might be able to find a drink or two. Plus, you're probably wearing four different Disney-related items of clothing when you head out for the park. As for sleep, well, if you're a parent of young children, I'm guessing that's already optional.

> You scream, I scream, we all scream extra loudly for ice cream, especially when it's the Kitchen Sink from the *Beaches 'n' Cream Soda Shop* at the Beach Club Resort. After I eat this amazing concoction with my family, I typically sit slumped in my chair with glazed eyes, to the point where after the server asks if I'm ok, I can only nod slowly, still floating somewhere in ice cream bliss. Here's a quick description of what's in it from the Disney website: "Scoops of Vanilla, Chocolate, Strawberry, Cookies 'n Cream, and Mint Chocolate Chip topped with Hot Fudge, Peanut Butter, SNICKERS® pieces, Fresh-baked Brownie, and smothered in every additional topping we have. Also available Chocolate Lovers or Neapolitan." If you go to Disney World and get this, let me know if you also had to be asked by the server if you were ok, and if so, if you were able to do anything besides nod. I'll be impressed.

Safety (security, protection from the elements): You just walked through the security screening at the "back entrance" of EPCOT, via the International Gateway. In the park, Disney obviously has its own security team and procedures. Plus, one of Disney's focus areas in training for all their Cast Members and throughout the parks is safety for guests and, of course, for the Cast Members themselves. So, you're probably in good shape on this need, as long as you use common sense. As for protection from the elements, you know they're doing some amazing things with Disney ponchos now, don't you?

Love and belonging (friendship, trust, love, being part of a group): You may be with family or friends or both on your trip—and possibly a significant other. And though I never like to assume, I'm guessing there's some love and trust and acceptance involved in these relationships. And you also likely feel part of an even larger group, such as the people around you at the specific attraction, overall around the park, and even larger still at the entire Disney World resort. And of course, as any Disney fan will tell you, you probably feel love for, and history with, the Disney characters and attractions you're seeing and experiencing.

Esteem (for oneself, for acceptance): There are many ways to achieve something important at a Disney park like EPCOT. Like my oldest son Jeremy, who got to dive with sea turtles, stingrays, sharks, and other creatures in the 5.7 million gallon saltwater aquarium at The Seas with Nemo & Friends Pavilion (formerly The Living Seas Pavilion). Or you can learn more about the planet so you can protect it on *Living with the Land*. And you might feel an enhanced sense of acceptance as you stand in the queue at *Test Track* wearing your interactive *Ratatouille* chef hat ("toque"), as Remy pops out the top, knowing no one is judging anyone, even a middle-aged accountant, for wearing a wacky hat at a Disney park. Why are they not? Because, at Disney, wacky hats are just hats.

Cognitive (knowledge, curiosity): It's basically impossible to visit a Disney park, especially EPCOT, and not learn something. In fact, many somethings. The Worlds of Discovery, Celebration, and Nature—and the World Showcase pavilions, like so much at Disney, combine entertainment and education so seamlessly that you can't quite tell if you're laughing while you're learning or the other way around.

Aesthetic (appreciation, search for beauty): From the architecture to the landscaping to the smells to the music to the art to the food to the lagoon, everywhere you turn at EPCOT, there's something to be appreciated. And every attraction and restaurant and pavilion and store and tree and flower hold their own special beauty, whether it's the queue in *Frozen Ever After*, the *Canada Far & Wide* movie, a chocolate and hazelnut Beignet from *Les Halles Boulangerie-Patisserie* in the France Pavilion, a fun and imaginative display of *Spaceship Earth* cookie jars at the Connections store, or simply standing in child-like amazement, watching the miniature trains of the Garden Railway near the Germany Pavilion make their way through towns and tunnels.

Self-actualization (realizing personal potential): It's easy to find something or someone that connects to your passion and purpose at a Disney park. Maybe you want to learn more about the history of communication on *Spaceship Earth*, or the mystery of the world's oceans in The Seas with Nemo & Friends Pavilion, or different civilizations and cultures at the World Showcase pavilions. Maybe your passion is experiencing music and art during EPCOT's Festival of the Arts. Or maybe you dream of one day designing cars, so you especially enjoy the queue at *Test Track*. As young Ellie tells young Carl in *Up*, "Adventure is out there!"

Transcendence (mystical experiences): If you're looking for mystical experiences, you've come to the right place, where mystery and wonder wait around every corner—whether you're flying on *Flight of Passage*, seeing Cinderella Castle for the first time, or wondering how you just exited your rebel shuttle on *Rise of the Resistance* into a Star Destroyer through the same door you entered (you didn't notice being turned around?). Or watching as a lion paces a rock ledge majestically on the *Kilimanjaro Safari*, or standing with thousands of other families, children and grandchildren sitting on shoulders, faces all bathed in torchlight, watching the music and fireworks show at the World Showcase Lagoon. And it's basically impossible not to get goosebumps when your "Time Machine" on *Spaceship Earth* begins to rotate at the top of the attraction, turning you towards Earth up above, and you hear Dame Judi Dench grandly say, "After 30,000 years of time travel, here we are—a truly global community, poised to shape the future of this, our Spaceship Earth." And, of course, the look on a child's face as their favorite Disney character signs their autograph book, which is really the best of all.

And of course, as all these needs are fulfilled, we *feel* something, don't we? We know how it feels to be safe and secure. We can tell when we love and are loved, when we belong and are accepted. We have all felt the thrill of learning something new, of seeing beauty, and of feeling like we're doing the thing we were put here to do. And I'm guessing most of us have felt a tear or a goosebump, or both, when witnessing something wondrous. The things that, to quote Hamlet in William Shakespeare's *Hamlet*, make us believe that "there are more things on heaven and earth, Horatio, then are dreamt of in your philosophy."

Yes, that all can happen with Disney. And does.

As it did for me on *Flight of Passage*.

Of course, this being a book about both the magic *and* the method, I'm not asking you to just take my word for it. Instead, let's hear from three people from three different backgrounds—an ambassador, a star of stage and screen, and a dream maker—to make the case with me.

An ambassador, a star, and a dream maker all walk into a room

First, the ambassador.

Or a former Disney Ambassador, to be exact.

Christopher White, a former Disney Ambassador and now a board member of the Disney Hometown Museum in Marceline, Missouri, addressed the importance of Disney in our lives after I asked if he agreed with my hypothesis that if Disney didn't exist, we'd need to create it.

After pausing for a moment, he answered (and, for bonus points, see how he covers Maslow's hierarchy as he does):

"Yes, Disney fills many of our needs. For example, reality is challenging, and we all need an escape from it at times. Of course, this applies when we're dealing with serious issues, like health and finances, but it can also be just an escape from our everyday life, where everything has become more complex.

"We feel a sense of hope with Disney, a place where we can go and have our spirits lifted, and where we can remember the goodness of people, including those from different walks of life, countries, and cultures.

"Disney also helps us feel like we belong. For me, personally, as a boy, I always had a passion for Disney, but didn't want to talk about it much, worried that people would think I was weird. But when I started working for Disney, I saw so much diversity that made me feel like I was part of something bigger. I have seen how Disney has been intentional about including everyone, making them feel the magic no matter their backgrounds, physical or mental abilities, where they're from, and so on.

"Just as important, the world seems to be separated into sides more than ever now. And, for most people who are really into Disney, it's something that bonds them, a common bond that allows people to put aside a lot of their other stuff."

Next up, a star.

Neil Patrick Harris, the aforementioned star of stage and screen and, well, just about everything else, is also a self-proclaimed admirer, devotee, and fan of Disney.

We had the privilege of seeing Neil Patrick Harris narrate Disney World's 2022 Candlelight Processional, a recounting of the Biblical story of Christmas, accompanied by an orchestra and large choir (which includes Disney Cast Members). According to mickeyblog. com, the Processional was first introduced at Disneyland in 1958, then Disney World in 1971, where it was initially located at the Magic Kingdom and then moved to EPCOT in 1994. It takes place during EPCOT's International Festival of the Holidays. Harris has narrated the event multiple times. And when we saw him, I'm not ashamed to say it was like seeing The Beatles, just with slightly shorter hair.

In his wonderful autobiography, *Neil Patrick Harris: Choose Your Own Autobiography*, Neil references how, as a child, his parents would take him and his brother out of school for a week every year to drive cross-country to Disneyland. His words (and, again, notice the hierarchy showing up), "And you fell utterly, *spiritually* (his italics), in love with the park. There is no bit of Disney magic that doesn't enchant you."

Then, from his grown-up perspective, he writes about going on *Peter Pan's Flight* with his husband and their two-year-old twins. "They both squeal with delight...You experience them experiencing pure magic...And as the ride makes its full circle, so do you, until Peter Pan has done it again, and you are once more a child, taking it all in, amazed, overwhelmed, enchanted."

Spiritually in love. Magic. Amazed. Overwhelmed. Enchanted.

Or dare we say, "transcendent."

And, finally, the dream maker.

Stephanie Schweigert is a reservation and ticketing coordinator with Give Kids The World Village® (GKTW), someone who helps make dreams come true for critically ill children.

After being introduced to GKTW by Brian Collins, a former Imagineer and someone you'll hear from later in the book, I was immediately struck by how much the Village also "hits" all of Maslow's levels. To see how both GKTW and Disney do this, let's listen to Stephanie's story:

"A few years back," Stephanie explains, "my husband and I, who lived in Minnesota at the time, were lucky enough to be able to adopt our daughters from foster care. All my children have complex needs, but my one daughter has Spina Bifida and Hydrocephalus. During her adoption process, their adoption worker told me about the Village. From there, we were referred to a local Minnesota Wish-granting organization, named Wishes and More, that helped connect us with the Village.

"When my daughter learned that she was eligible for a Wish trip, she immediately wanted to go to the Village and Disney World. There was no other wish that came close for her, especially because she was obsessed with the Disney princesses.

"There are so many moments I remember from that trip with my family to Disney World. The biggest of all was when I was able to get a picture of my three daughters in their princess dresses in front of Cinderella Castle. The Disney photographer and other Cast Members saw their GKTW buttons and treated them so special, giving them extra time and personalized magic. That included the photographer taking their individual pictures and then photos with the group.

"The other special moment was to see my Wish child, who was afraid of many things, getting an embrace from Snow White and then suddenly not being so scared anymore, opening up to new things, enjoying the entire trip with our family.

"Looking back, during that whole week, while her doctors provided her medicine, it was the magic of GKTW and Disney that healed her in so many ways. Knowing how happy we were at both places, we actually decided to move down to Florida, close to both places."

With that, it's easy to see why we fall in love with Disney.

So, the next question is, "Now that we believe in the storyteller, what story will they tell?"

Questions

1. What's your Disney "origin" story? When did it first become part of your life?

2. If you are, when did you fall in love with Disney? Any ideas on what did the trick?

3. How many Disney items, including clothing, movies, music, artwork, etc., do you have? Feel free to "guesstimate" if it's above 14,350.

4. When have you felt wonder in your life? Did you ever feel that with Disney?

5. What's the one Disney souvenir that holds the greatest meaning for you? Why?

2 Everything Starts with Story

"You are not the first to pass this way. Nor shall you be the last. Those who seek the spirit of Norway face peril and adventure——but more often, find beauty and charm..."

Opening Narration from *Maelstrom*,
former Disney attraction

Remembering this opening narration from the now-retired *Maelstrom* boat "dark ride" attraction (now *Frozen Ever After*, which incorporates a few elements of the former ride) in the Norway Pavilion at EPCOT always takes me back. In fact, even just then, as I was typing the words for the chapter lead-in, they got to me. I heard the mysterious, commanding voice in my head.

They bring back a place and a time and a feeling.

As they also apparently did for participants in a *How Does Disney Do That?* workshop last year. Theron and I were presenting to The Carolwood Society in the GM Conference and Training Center at *Test Track* in EPCOT. At one point, to illustrate the power of Disney's storytelling, I asked the participants to close their eyes and then raise their hands if they recognized the words I was about to share. As I guessed, I only had to say the first five or so, "You are not the first..." before hands shot up. And as they did, I heard excited whispering and even a few exclamations, attesting to the lasting impact of the attraction and the ability of those words of invitation to...

...take them back.

According to carolwood.com, The Carolwood Society is dedicated to preserving the personal railroad legacy of Walt Disney. The society was co-founded by Michael Broggie and his wife, Sharon. Michael is a Disney historian and speaker, and author of *Walt Disney's Railroad Story*. He is also the son of Roger E. Broggie, Walt Disney's first Imagineer. This book includes a story from Michael and other members of the society. I'm grateful for their support.

As they also do for my family. Right back to our many visits to Disney World as our children were growing up, where we'd often start at the Mexico Pavilion in EPCOT. There, after a meal at the *San Angel Inn Restaurante*, which sits just beyond a beautiful recreation of a colorful Mexican village and marketplace at twilight, and a ride on *El Rio del Tiempo* (now *Gran Fiesta Tour Starring the Three Caballeros*), we'd make our much-anticipated visit to *Maelstrom*.

After looking for Hidden Mickeys in the queue's wall murals that foreshadowed the ride's events, we climbed into our "Viking boat." As the opening narration accompanied our climb, rotating beams of light pierced the darkness, coming from the eye of "Odin" at the top of the hill—a character based on the mythological Norse god of the same name.

Just over the crest, we gently dropped a few feet into a Norwegian story that spanned a thousand years. One that took us past an ancient seafaring town, with Viking ships moving through churning seas between fire-tipped mountains, until we met up with angry trolls, including a three-headed troll who cast a spell on us, yelling, "Disappear, back, back, over the falls!"

As the spell worked, the back of our boat pivoted to the right and we shot backwards down another hill, past a towering polar bear with a menacing roar. At the bottom of that drop, after our boat came to a jolting stop (something guests would see from outside the attraction), the *front* of our boat then pivoted to the right, and we plummeted forward down another hill, onto the surface of the "North Sea." Relieved to be just a little wet, but a whole lot excited, we then floated past several oil platforms, and ended up in a quaint, but decidedly more modern, Norwegian fishing village.

So, what was the most memorable part of the ride? The Vikings? The trolls? The backward plunge? Getting wet as we slammed into the North Sea? Well, those were all great, but no.

The most memorable part, for me, was the very beginning when we first heard, "You are not the first to pass this way..."

Why?

Because for me, it's like a child hearing "Once upon a time..." from their favorite bedtime story—an invitation to another time and place, like Tinkerbell from long ago, sprinkling her pixie dust across my TV.

Plus, because that narration had become so much a part of our family, every time we heard it, whether we were at Disney World or back in the "Real World," it reminded us of all the times we'd heard it before, what we'd been doing then, how we felt on that first day of our trip, and so on. Just like when we'd take our kids' picture in front of the fountain at the Morocco Pavilion on every trip. When we look at those pictures now, it's the Disney version of pencil marks on a child's height chart. They mark the moments.

Yes, that is what great stories, told by great storytellers, do. Take us back, invite us in, and mark the time.

"Michael Lyons, author of *Drawn to Greatness: Disney's Animation Renaissance*, former Disney leader, and co-host of the podcasts *Dis-Order: Every Disney Film* and *From Pencils to Pixels: The Animation Celebration Podcast*, shared one of his family's Disney stories:

"I became a Disney fan partly because my dad was such a big Disney fan. He saw *Snow White and the Seven Dwarfs* in 1938, when he was four, at Radio City Music Hall, and would tell me about that (and how the Wicked Queen scared him so much, he almost ran out of the theater).

"He passed his passion for Disney on to me, and we eventually made our first visit to Walt Disney World in 1987. My first clear memory of that trip was when my dad and I walked through the train station tunnel at the Magic Kingdom onto Main Street.

"As soon as we did, my dad turned to me and said, 'We're here!' And that is when my Disney story really began."

The story of the story

Disney, the storyteller we came to believe in and love in Chapter One, always starts with story. One we already care about or soon will.

Then they give it flesh and form.

By adding layer upon layer of carefully designed and executed detail, even details that appear random, in a way that makes it feel real and sincere.

By adding characters we care about—heroes, heroines, sidekicks, villains, and their sidekicks, and, of course, it never hurts to have some soldiers and townspeople in there, too. Oh, and lots and lots of singing (and possibly sewing) animals. And, of course, there are sometimes parents; though, in a Disney movie, if you're a parent, I wouldn't recommend you put too much into your 401(k) plan.

Plus, a horse. Yes, a horse always seems to save the day.

Want an example of just how important horses are to Disney? Well, the refurbished lobby of the Saratoga Springs Resort at Disney World is surrounded by large paintings featuring horses from Disney and Pixar movies. While there one day, a Cast Member quizzed my wife and me on the names of the horses and the movies they were in. Some might say my wife trounced me in that quiz. And those "some" would very well be right. But I do believe there was something in my eye during that quiz, otherwise it would have been much closer.

Adam Berger, author of *Every Guest is a Hero: Disney's Theme Parks and the Magic of Mythic Storytelling*, independent contractor/show writer for Walt Disney Imagineering, and owner of Berger Creative Associates, shares his perspective on how Disney approaches storytelling:

"Disney has a laser-like focus on storytelling that positively impacts the guest experience. In fact, like James, I was reminded of this the first time I rode on *Flight of Passage*. One of the most amazing things about the attraction is the beauty of its imagery, and how it seamlessly blends visuals with motion, music, and sound effects—along with the sounds of the banshee breathing under you, its wings flapping, other creatures, the wind and water, all of it.

"When it was over, I remember a voice in my head crying 'No!' I didn't want it to end and go back to real life. It also made me think about the story behind the attraction, which ties back to my work as an independent show writer for Disney.

"So, what does a show writer at Disney do?

"Well, they often function as the guardian of the story, which at Walt Disney Imagineering may sometimes include developing a 'Show Information Guide.' The guide tells the design story of an attraction, retail or dining venue, themed land, or even an entire park. It acts as an archival document, too, helping everyone know the thought process that went into developing that attraction or venue. It is also very helpful for training new Cast Members and educating outside contractors if changes or additions are needed down the line. For me, the document is also a great opportunity to look 'under the hood'—to see the creative process, how the story came together and was expressed through color design, lighting, landscaping, costumes, signage, graphics, etc., all the components that make an experience three-dimensional and immersive."

Next, Disney sprinkles in the spice: jokes, drama, suspense, adventure, songs, color, and more.

The end result? That we believe in make-believe.

As gradually, and suddenly, as falling in love.

So, how do we know the impact a storyteller and their story can have on us? Well, to answer that, for just a moment, let's leave Disney to attend the morning session of a typical corporate conference, and then, later that same day, listen in as a parent reads a bedtime story to their child.

First, let's fly, Peter Pan style, of course, to attend part of a conference in San Diego for a large pharmaceutical company—and let's pop in on the most complex (read: for me, boring) sessions, filled with an executive referring for over an hour to 6pt font financials, flowcharts, and process maps. While there, let's also steal a glance at the other participants in the darkened conference hall.

What do we see? Many are covertly and not-so-covertly looking down at their phones, scrolling through social feeds, texting, or checking email. We also see a yawn or two. Plus, we notice how many of them are sitting way back in their seats, slightly slumped from the too-heavy-because-the-company-paid-for-it lunch they had (though they're also already thinking about what the afternoon snack might be).

But then, *it* happens.

Another executive takes the stage, and we can tell right away that she's different. She seems to have more energy. And, instead of opening by talking about the year-to-date trends, she turns to the audience and...shares a personal story.

About her Uber ride from the airport where she learned something surprising about her driver that she wanted to share with the group. How the driver is driving for Uber, in addition to his regular job, to make enough money to start a caregiver support business. And when the leader tells the story, she shares details. Lots of them. The color of the car. The excitement in the driver's voice when he talked about his goal. How he wants to focus on caregivers because he and his wife have a young daughter with special needs. The photo of the daughter proudly Scotch-taped near the car radio. Even the song that was on the radio as they talked (*Reminiscing* by the Little River Band). And with each detail, the audience is invited deeper into the story.

Now, what if we looked back around at the session's participants at *that* moment? What would we see? Well, from many years of speaking, teaching speaking, and evaluating speakers, I can tell you confidently that many of those phones would be gone, shoved hastily back into pockets or bags, as their owners leaned in to listen. And, at the same time, many would have shifted forward in their seats. Plus, the air itself would feel like it had subtly changed, filled with more zap and sizzle. You could likely hear a pin drop. Very small, lightweight pins.

And if you had to guess at how that audience felt right then? More energetic, for sure, because as any speaker—really, anyone on stage—knows, you get what you give. Oh, and they're likely curious, wanting to see how the leader will connect the lessons she learned during the conversation with her driver back to the conference, the company, and—most importantly—them.

Why did their attention and attitude change? Because they were invited into a story by a storyteller who obviously cared. And so, because they then cared, too, it was an invitation they gladly accepted.

That's one example of how stories change us. Now, let's look at another.

For this one, let's take one more Peter Pan flight (with a lay-over this time to make the whole trip a bit more economical) to Minnesota, to listen in as a six-year-old girl asks, "Mommy, will you read me a bedtime story?"

Mom sighs, but to herself, so her daughter doesn't hear. She's exhausted from a long day of teaching at the high school, followed by a long evening of making dinner, grading tests, playing "Candyland" with her daughter three times after giving her a bath, and then watching an episode of their favorite TV show together. But, knowing that there will come a day soon when she'd give anything to have her daughter ask her to read her a bedtime story, she agrees, tucks her into bed, and begins. "Once upon a time, there was a magical princess..."

And right then, her daughter smiles and snuggles deeper under her blanket and into her pillow. Then, to make the moment even better, once the story starts the girl realizes that her mom is making *her* the center of it! *She* is the magical princess on a quest to save her village, while battling several dragons and other horned beasts along the way—all while wearing a tiara, of course.

In a few minutes, as the little girl's eyelids slowly droop, as her breathing deepens, the mom fades the story out, ending with a whispered "happily ever after." She leans over and kisses her daughter on the cheek.

In the end, then, what does that story do for the little girl? Well, she's the focus of her mother's attention, which makes her feel cared about. And, because she loves her mom, the storyteller, and feels safe in her own bed, she's more likely to believe, let go, and imagine. Spellbound, if you will.

And for the mom? Well, after turning on her daughter's night light and quietly closing her bedroom door, the mom stops in the hall...and smiles, not feeling as stressed anymore and thankful that she didn't miss that special time with her daughter, something she knows she would have regretted later.

The people we love, we give time to, like sharing a story with a child. To understand this feeling, it might also be helpful to remember someone else who talked to children in a way that made them feel special, noticed, and cared about.

Mr. Fred Rogers.

Remember how he used to talk to us? Remember the stories he told, and the way he and Trolley transported us on the TV series *Mr. Rogers' Neighborhood* into the "Land of Make-Believe," a colorful world of kings and queens and a variety of wonderful animals—like owls, and tigers, and pussycats, and more—where lessons were learned but in such a fun way that we didn't even know we were learning them? Lessons about love, and acceptance, and how to deal with the harder parts of life, like loneliness and grief?

And, really, wasn't there something about the way Mr. Rogers talked to children in a direct and caring way that reminds us of how Walt did the same?

Yes, stories transform. The teller. The told. And even the tale itself.

As it did with me on *Flight of Passage*. Turned me back into a wide-eyed little boy who believed that, for a moment, he was actually in flight. A belief made possible through the Disney Imagineers and others from Disney who helped make a banshee and those Pandoran skies feel as safe and magical as a bedtime story bed.

Disney does that.

Ladies and gentlemen, may I please introduce...

Now, as mentioned earlier, after riding *Flight of Passage* and writing about the experience, I connected with Theron Skees, a former Walt Disney Imagineering (WDI) creative executive with over 23 years of WDI experience, and now founder of The Designer's Creative Studio. I also mentioned how you'd be hearing from him throughout the book through "Theron's Keys," a collection of his stories and insights about creating experiences that create feelings.

Why "Theron's Keys" for these sections? Well, that's a funny story! You'd think it's just my clever take (you know, because I'm humbly brilliant) on Theron's name. And you'd be right. Partly.

But I can't really take the credit for it. No, it's mostly inspired by the creative team that worked with Theron on the transformation of Downtown Disney at Disney World into Disney Springs. That's because, if you walk into *Jock Lindsey's Hangar Bar* at Disney Springs (the fictional Jock Lindsey piloted Indiana

Jones' plane in the opening scene of *Raiders of the Lost Ark*) and turn to your right just before the bar starts, and right again, you'll see a cage in the wall featuring "Lost and Found" items.

Among those items are some keys hanging on a board on the wall on the left. You'll see a key labelled "Theron S." Why? Because Theron played a "key" oversight creative role in the transformation of the Springs and his last name has "kee" in it.

So, what you're really seeing hanging there is Theron S.' Key. Get it?

Oh, yes, and if you walk towards the back of the restaurant and peek inside the replica of the "bathysphere" submersible vehicle, then look slightly up, you'll see a black and white photo of a man in a diving suit surrounded by a dive team. That dive team? Yep, more of the creative Disney people who worked with Theron on the Springs. And the man in the diving suit? Well, I'm guessing you know the answer to that now...

Want to see both of these items but don't have time to hop a plane to Orlando? Go to my *How Does Disney Do That?* group on Facebook and search *Jock Lindsey's Hangar Bar.*

Oh, and one more thing, there is a table in that bathysphere where people eat. So, if you do poke your head in, and they wonder why, just mention this book. They should then nod knowingly, especially once it sells over seven million copies. In the first month.

So, with that, when I asked Theron about the power of story at Disney and how it helps create an emotional connection with their guests, this is what he shared.

Theron's Keys #1: "Happily Ever After" is planned

It doesn't happen accidentally; there is purpose behind all of it. And it always starts with the story and its narrative. Like the stories that take place in books, TV, movies, theme parks and other entertainment, augmented reality, and more. And that narrative structure works because it's been with us for so long, whether it's cave paintings, Greek mythology, or Shakespearean monologues. As humans, one of the core ways we communicate is through story. And with stories come feelings.

At Disney, there's a long heritage of telling emotionally-rich stories, so we plan to bring out certain feelings in guests.

For example, many people watch a movie, see a TV show, read a book, or go to the theater or a theme park, and have a natural emotional response to it. When they do, they may feel like it simply happened to them out of the blue. They might not think about how that emotional reaction may have been planned and *hoped* for—meaning that experience designers worked to make sure that just the right content and conditions came together to make that feeling more likely.

Yes, we planned for it, by creating stories with such detail that they conveyed a real place and time, even if that place and time had never actually existed. Our goal was then to use that realism to get guests to suspend their disbelief long enough to believe in the story and feel that they were part of it.

A story also needs to be told in such a way that people of different ages, from different cultures and backgrounds, and with different expectations, can still all find themselves in it. For them, some of these stories might be aspirational, some may give them glimpses of things that have happened in their lives, and many are often about redemption. Because in a sense, all of us are seeking a type of redemption within our own lives.

Of course, in a Disney story, an underdog often takes on the "Hero's Journey," and matures and grows along the way while encountering difficulties. They overcome great challenges and face their greatest fears while they learn, adapt, and often, learn to love and be loved. Obviously, all emotional moments.

And of course, that emotional component is why story is so important at Disney. Yes, if you just go to an amusement park and jump on a roller coaster, that's a thrilling experience. It's fun. It taps into our human need for escapism and play because you can't do that in your backyard, and you can't do that in your normal everyday activity.

But when people really *enter* a story like James did on *Flight of Passage*, then there's a real emotional connection available. Because it demonstrates that, even though part of our brain tells us that it's artificial, we can suspend disbelief for a while and allow another belief to begin—the one unfolding in front of us, one that we want to be part of.

So in this case, after James sat down next to his son and put on those goggles, he dropped into a very real, very organic world. As he described earlier, his disbelief was so suspended that he wasn't even thinking that what he was seeing was actually a very well-done digital film. No, in his brain and heart, he immediately accepted it as real.

According to orias.berkeley.edu, Joseph Campbell's Monomyth, developed in *Hero with a Thousand Faces*, describes the common heroic narrative (or "Hero's Journey") in which a heroic protagonist sets out, has transformative adventures, and returns home.

Want another example of how a storyteller and their story can emotionally engage an audience?

Just look at how some *Avatar* fans felt after they watched James Cameron's movie and had to go back to real life. To get a sense for the depth of the connection formed and the possible double-edged nature of that connection—when fans suspend disbelief to become part of a story but then have a hard time suspending that suspension—just do an online search of "How did fans feel after *Avatar* was over?" Powerful stuff.

Which makes me think about my own reactions, though much more muted, when Disney attractions, shows, and events I care about change or go away. Or when a Disney trip ends, and we have to go home. That's, of course, the other side of love.

Ok, let's stop for a minute, grab a Disney churro, and talk about where we are right now.

To recap, we've confirmed that we're in love with Disney, the storyteller, why we're in love, and how that love makes it much more possible that we'll believe in their story enough to become part of it.

So, what's next? What comes after we accept the invitation and take the storyteller's hand? What will make us "Let It

Go" and leave reality for fantasy enough so that the fantasy *becomes* reality?

The details.

Questions

1. What's your favorite narration from a Disney attraction?

2. If you've gone on multiple Disney vacations, do you always start in the same park? In the same place? On the same attraction? Or, in the same part of the Disney Cruise ship? If so, why?

3. Who is your favorite character and sidekick from a Disney book, cartoon, or movie? That will say a *lot* about you. (Mine are Donald Duck from the cartoons and Pascal from *Tangled*. From those two pieces of information, you now know everything there is to know about me.)

4. What Disney song do you like the most? (And for extra bonus points, will you join one of my *How Does Disney Do That?* online groups and post a video of yourself singing it?)

5. If you were ever in a boring presentation or lecture (ok, I know, we have all been in them), what effect would it have on you if the speaker started by sharing a personal story?

3   Details Are the Doorway

"When making experiences, attention to detail matters."

Richard Branson, Founder of the Virgin Group

I t's wonderful when you notice the details with Disney.

But it's even better when you don't.

As we go from being enchanted by a story to forgetting we're even in one—transforming as we cross the transom.

Of course, saying that Disney's in the details is like saying the sky is blue. But, because it's easy to take the sky being blue for granted, it's also important to recognize this simple but amazing fact every so often.

To appreciate it.

Now, my family, like most, has appreciated the details Disney offers for as long as we've been fans, especially those details that would be so easy to rush right on by. Where, when you do notice them, it's like stumbling upon a little treasure, something that, for the moment, is just for you.

Such as...

...Our boat on *Gran Fiesta Tour Starring the Three Caballeros* at the Mexico Pavilion in EPCOT started out, gliding past a pyramid and erupting volcano on the left, and, just beyond the railing, the *San Angel Inn Restaurante* on the right. No matter how many times we've ridden, it's always wonderful to feel like you're isolated deep in the jungle on one side and waving to diners on the other, their faces flickering in the light of their table lamps. But for me, the best detail of that opening sequence is the small thatched hut near the base of the pyramid. Why? Because it wasn't really necessary. With the water, boat, pyramid, volcano, jungle, and restaurant, the Imagineers could have "taken five," in my eyes, and not added it. Or, at a minimum, they could have made it not quite as detailed as it is, with a light shining from the inside, where you can imagine a meal cooking upon a fire. So easy to miss or take for granted...if you're not paying attention.

...We walked through Radiator Springs at Disney California Adventure Park at the Disneyland Resort, with its rocky out-croppings and mountain ranges named after Cadillac fins rising in the distance, past *Luigi's*, *Flo's V8 Café*, *Mater's Junk-yard*, and the *Cozy Cone Motel*. And if anyone ever tells you that lighting can't make you feel something, I have one word for them: neon.

...Our boat on *Living with the Land* in The Land Pavilion at EPCOT made its way through a deciduous forest in a rain-storm, thunder rumbling in the distance, while water rushed down rivulets between the tree roots...then through a rain forest, past alligators and a pounding waterfall...and later a midwestern American farmhouse, framed by a brilliant sun-rise, with a dog barking on the porch, a swing hanging from a tree, and a rooster sitting on the mailbox. But the best detail is the one you can't see from the boat: a secret bedroom on the second floor of that farmhouse.

Have you ever seen the secret bedroom on the second floor of the farmhouse on the *Living with the Land* attraction at The Land Pavil-ion at EPCOT? If not, the next time you happen to be at the *Garden Grill* restaurant, which slowly rotates a floor above the attraction, watch carefully as you go past the farmhouse. You'll see a furnished bedroom on the top floor facing you, complete with an antique globe, quilt-covered bed, gas lights, and more. Just think about that for a second. The Imagineers put all that time and attention into doing something that most people wouldn't even know was there, just so a small group of people could discover it!

...Turned the corner onto the Streets of America at Disney's Hollywood Studios to see the *Osborne Family Spectacle of Dancing Lights*. Over five million lights, an illuminated Earth accompanied by doves under a "Peace on Earth" sign, flying Santa and reindeer, spinning sky carousel, marching Tin Soldiers, and much more. All while "snow" was falling— *in Florida*!

To paraphrase the story from wdwmagic.com:

"*The Osborne Family Spectacle of Dancing Lights* was born at the Osborne home in Little Rock, Ark., in 1986. That year, Jennings Osborne strung a modest 1,000 red lights as a holiday gift to his 6-year-old daughter, 'Breezy.' Thus, a new tradition was born.

"...Osborne's dream kept growing until 1993, when he strung more than three million lights. His 22,000-square-foot home, bathed in bulbs, was the site of curious sightseers and long lines of traffic. Calling his display a nuisance, though, Osborne's neighbors took legal action—all the way to the Arkansas Supreme Court.

"Shortly after the court battle, Osborne packed his bulbs and took them to the Walt Disney World Resort..."

...Had dinner at the *Animator's Palate* restaurant on the second night of our cruise on the Disney *Wonder*, amazed as the entire restaurant, including the staff's uniforms, underwent a transformation from black and white to color. Adding to this, our same servers rotated along with our family to a different restaurant on successive nights, ensuring that, by the second night, we were all being addressed by name. Yes, details show up in the service, too.

...Smelled and saw the embers from the famous burning of the Library of Alexandria as Rome fell on *Spaceship Earth*—along with smelling the Disney resorts as soon as we walked into their lobbies, each with its own unique scent (our particular favorites were the Beach Club Resort and Coronado Springs Resort). As my wife points out, they were scents we often smelled even before we could take in the lobby by sight. And of course, the more details affect all five senses, the more likely they are to affect the sixth.

...Noticed how details were embedded even in the sidewalks and walkways of the Disney World resorts and attractions, including animal prints leading up to the Wilderness Resort and Lodge, foliage imprints sunk into the sidewalk in front of the Kidani Village at the Animal Kingdom Resort, and Andy's huge footprints stamped into the concrete path of Toy Story Land at Disney's Hollywood Studios. (For more examples, just go to your favorite browser and type in "Disney Sidewalk Details" and watch how many items come up—about looking down!)

...Buying my wife the "Laila Eau de Parfum" from the gift shop in the Norway Pavilion because, well, I love to smell it on her, and that's just about everything I'm going to say about that right here...

...As we walked through the beautifully detailed queue of *Flight of Passage*, sat upon our so-life-like-I-thought-I-had-to-feed-mine banshees, and dropped into the skies of Pandora over forests and oceans and every animal imaginable on an imaginary world that, for a time, became anything but.

Theron's Keys #2: A lot of planning is needed to make it feel like it wasn't planned at all

Human beings absorb the details around them, and those details convey realism. The more they can recognize details from other places or times in a Disney attraction or show, the more it helps them become immersed. Those details can also help bring order and give them comfort through the familiar.

The level of planning that goes into those details is often far beyond what you'd imagine. For example, when we were working on the transformation of Downtown Disney into Disney Springs, we needed to think about how to create a life-like Florida spring (the largest body of water Disney has ever made) that would remain colorful, even under the Florida sun, and that would not necessitate draining the waterway to keep it maintained.

To start, we knew we needed to make it out of the most durable material possible, with the longest lifecycle. So we ended up using pebble technology with pigmented concrete and different shades of glass. But the manufacturer had never applied it with the variety of colors we needed, so to really know what it would look like and how it would perform, it had to be tested underwater.

So we went to the water. The Typhoon Lagoon waterpark. At 3am.

Every day, for weeks, we'd put panels with the pigmented concrete into the large pool at Typhoon Lagoon, tow them around to different depths, and then pull them out so Cast Members could get the park ready for the guests later that morning.

What's the response we're looking for from guests to the spring? Well, often, the best response is no response, with them believing it's real. Because if we've suspended your disbelief so completely, transported you so successfully, that you've simply enjoyed yourselves and didn't recognize the difference between real and designed, then we've done our job.

Another great example of detail is the steam water pump in Disney Springs that's off to the side, at the *Sprinkles* location beside *Frontera Cocina* and across the springs from *Raglan Road Irish Restaurant and Pub*. The pump reinforces the story that fresh spring water was originally pumped into the "Icehouse" to make block ice. This is important because, though Disney Springs isn't a theme park, Disney still added that level of storytelling to a retail, dining, and entertainment destination!

Just as important, at all locations, we don't want guests to realize the artificiality of the details, like knocking on a column and noticing it's hollow. For me, for example, whenever I'm talking specifically about Disney Springs, I explain that we used all natural materials, because in my career I had seen so many people walking up to columns of buildings that were meant to look like stone, knocking on them, hearing they were hollow, and being taken out of the story of that attraction or venue.

That moment can rip them out of the story, especially if it happens repeatedly, or affects many of the senses, like the shiny penny in

Somewhere in Time. That's why at Disney, if you grab a door handle on Main Street, it's bronze. Or, if something is supposed to be brass, it's brass. It feels real. And it reinforces that you're in this particular time period or fantasy world, and helps you remain in the story.

The same goes with music at the parks and the psychology that goes into it. For example, if you examine the entrance music to the Disney theme parks, up to a certain point in the day it's typically mostly ascending scales and keys and uplifting rhythms, to reinforce an optimistic, welcoming approach. Then in the evening, because people begin to leave the park, it switches and does the exact opposite, with descending notes to make it feel like a warm goodbye. We don't want it to be abrupt, but rather to gently escort you out with a goodnight kiss.

Most important, it's all done so subconsciously that very few people could actually put a finger on it. But those subconscious elements woven into the story are so important to the welcoming message as you enter and the kiss goodbye as you leave...

Because overall, when you enter a Disney theme park, it's the establishment, or re-establishment, of a very important relationship. You're welcoming an old friend in the morning and then later that day you're saying, 'See you next time!' And in between those moments is a choreographed experience...and that is the difference between a theme park and an amusement park."

In the movie *Somewhere in Time*, Christopher Reeve plays a Chicago playwright who travels back in time from 1980 to 1912 through self-hypnosis to meet an actress, played by Jane Seymour, who is appearing at the Grand Hotel on Mackinac Island in Michigan. For this to work, he must remove all reminders of his current time from his clothes and hotel room. But after he successfully travels back and they fall in love, he accidentally finds a shiny 1979 penny he had forgotten to remove in a small pocket of his suit. This instantly takes him out of the hypnotic state and returns him back to the modern year.

And, in the process, he made it impossible for any man, including myself, to impress his spouse. After all, how are you going to defend, "Well, Christopher Reeve traveled back in time for his love, then died because he couldn't get back to her, then met up with her again in the afterlife...but you couldn't take out the garbage?!"

What sets Disney details apart?

Disney details always serve the story. And I do mean *always.* The benches on *Tron Lightcycle / Run* at the Magic Kingdom fit the futuristic feel of the attraction. Cast Members receive backstories, as they did on *The Great Movie Ride*, for example, to help inform their roles. There's a tiny house built at the base of a tree trunk in Adventureland at Disneyland, said to be the home of Patrick Begorra, a leprechaun called the "Little Man of Disneyland." If there's a detail at Disney, it has a story behind it. If it doesn't, you're not at Disney.

Here's D23.com on the Little Man of Disneyland:

"The 'buried gold' of this elusive leprechaun begins with those fan-favorites, the Disney Little Golden Books. These well-told, richly illustrated volumes—both adaptations of classic films and specially created stories—were often illustrated by moonlighting Disney Studio artists, including such Disney Legends as John Hench, Al Dempster, and Mary Blair.

"In 1955, several Little Golden Books spun stories around Walt's latest dream-come-true, Disneyland. The most fantastical of these was Little Man of Disneyland, the charming story of Patrick, a leprechaun who lives in a tiny, half-hidden house at the roots of an Anaheim orange tree—until one day Donald Duck, Mickey Mouse, and Goofy (and Pluto, too) turn up. They are ready to start moving trees so they can build 'a wonderful place called Disneyland...with all sorts of marvelous things for fun.'

"The friends take the little man on a helicopter ride back to the Disney Studio—exactly how Walt traveled back and forth from Burbank—to see the Disneyland blueprints, drawings, and concept paintings (all based on actual Disneyland art). Patrick agrees to let them build the park—as long as he can live there in a new house. Once Disneyland is ready to open, Patrick moves into a 'wee snug house' of his own in a secret spot at the park known only to him."

Want to see a picture of the house? Go to the Disney Parks Blog online and search "The Little Man of Disneyland and His Adventureland Home."

They're authentic. Want to create a "Himalayan Escapes: Tours and Expeditions" travel agency for the *Expedition Everest: Legend of the Forbidden Mountain*? Well, then, go to Asia, see the Himalayas, visit the villages, meet the people, eat the food, take in their art, learn the way they live and work. Then bring as much of what you've learned back to the attraction.

They're layered. Like reading a "Seek and Find" children's book over and over, you can always find something new in Disney's attractions, resorts, restaurants, cruise ships, and more. With that amount of layering and complexity, the closer you look, the more you see. And every time you do find something new, you have a little more ownership of the experience, now being "in the know," and being able to share that special knowledge with others.

Think Hidden Mickeys, too.

They go beyond what's expected. See "small thatched hut" earlier.

They surround you. When we go on a Disney attraction, my family knows that at some point I will say, "I love looking where most people don't." So, if the ride is set up to encourage guests to look to the left, I look to the right, wondering just how far the Imagineers took the illusion. Because there's just no possible way they could have thought about that one guest in 100, like me, who would do that, correct? Well, wrong, of course. As you'd imagine, Disney doesn't just create a 180-degree experience.

They sometimes appear to simply be an unplanned effect of nature and time. Whether it's artificial rust, wear, or more, these are the details that really immerse guests, the ones we might just catch out of the corner of our eye, wondering how we ever thought they were real, until once again we forget they're not. As Theron has explained to me, Disney usually adds that patina of "age" to most places just so that it feels lived in.

They let us know someone cares. When I asked my wife how the details at Disney affect her, she said, "I feel valued. Like I matter enough for them to do that for me." And that, to me, perfectly describes my feeling after I came off *Flight of Passage* that first time. Someone, somewhere, had cared enough to put that time and attention into giving me *that* experience.

"When we would partner with Walt Disney Imagineering to design a new land or attraction, we always started with a story," said Dan Cockerell, author, consultant, and former VP of Disney's EPCOT, Hollywood Studios, and Magic Kingdom parks.

"And, although it was very detailed and many guests were never going to know all the details, the story aligned all the designers so they could be consistent and create something that just all came together.

"Part of telling that story was doing things like focusing on what the architecture would be. For example, when planning a new theater behind Main Street in the Magic Kingdom, the storyline we landed on was connected to Walt Disney's life in St. Louis in the 1940s.

"To prepare for that, the Imagineers went to St. Louis. Once there, they looked at different things that made up the 'style,' even the detail of the kind of bricks being used. Now, many guests may not recognize that level of detail and authenticity consciously, but somehow, they just know it makes sense.

"Most of all, everything is designed so that guests feel immersed in that storyline. That means thinking about what people will see, hear, smell, and touch in that story. Like, with touch, even the sidewalks are themed to help tell the story. Even the wallpaper and lighting play a part.

"It's also about removing or hiding anything that doesn't fit with the story, avoiding 'visual intrusion.' Like Walt's original direction that, once you're inside a park or land, all you should see is that area.

"Consider how language is used to reinforce the story by Cast Members in different lands. With Frontierland in the Magic Kingdom, you'll hear 'Howdy!' a lot. If you go to Tomorrowland, you'll hear, 'Welcome, space traveler.'

"A good example of the importance of 'backstory,' which is the story behind the story, was at the *Whispering Canyon* restaurant at the Wilderness Lodge. First, the name of the restaurant was a play on words because it's loud there—it's a big, open restaurant, and it opens into a large, open lobby. And the story is that all the people who work there were actually headed out west, but stopped at the restaurant along the way. Some of them were just passing through but decided to stay. When a new Cast Member joined the staff, we would ask them to give us their stage name and background story.

"So one Cast Member would say, 'I left New York and was making my way across the United States 'cause I wanted to open a ranch. Along the way, I found the *Whispering Canyon* and I'm here for a couple of months to make some money before I'm on my way again.'

"With Star Wars Galaxy's Edge at the Hollywood Studios Park, the idea is you have literally left Walt Disney World and gone to another planet. Once there, if you look at things like the costumes, you'll see that Disney has given the Cast Members the flexibility to have different patches and accessories to customize their look and make it appear much more non-uniform as it would likely be on another planet.

"When designing a new land, we would also have to think about the time period that land was set in and stay true to that. With Main Street, it's the turn-of-the-century—an era considered to be full of optimism and hope. So that's how we wanted guests to feel on Main Street as part of that story.

"Yes, that level of detail is key to telling a story. Why so much detail? Because, once again, when you give everyone on the design team a specific place in a specific time to focus their skills on, whether it's fictional or non-fictional, they're able to dive into details and do studies on it and really add those elements. And, as I said, though not all guests are going to notice, some might. Even for those who might not consciously notice, they're going to know that everything belongs, everything fits.

"In one of my favorite lands, Liberty Square at the Magic Kingdom, the attention to detail is fantastic. Look at the shutters on the buildings— they're all askew, a little off-kilter, because during the Revolutionary War they needed all the metal they could get for producing musket bullets. They took the hinges off the shutters and replaced them with leather. And of course, leather stretches with the weather. And so their being off-kilter is actually more accurate than if they were straight.

"The *Emporium* store on Main Street is another great example of that attention to detail and authenticity. If you go into the *Emporium*, you'll see chandeliers. Now, at the turn-of-the-century, chandeliers mostly ran on gas. They pointed up so that the flames could come out of the top.

Then, as electricity was more widely introduced, they added pieces of metal going down where they could put a lightbulb in. So in the *Emporium*, you'll see chandeliers originally designed for candles or gas but also with metal pieces for bulbs.

"And once again, a lot of guests won't notice all these details, but the designers do. And it just adds that little extra something that everyone knows is special. They may not know exactly what it is, but they can feel it."

The moment of magic

And then, when everything is just right, when the level of detail designed into the attraction or venue is so comprehensive and well-executed, and when we, the guests, are in just the right frame of mind and heart to let all that detail in—*that* is when it happens.

Transformation. Transcendence.

For me, this transcendence happened on *Flight of Passage*.

Remember Maslow? To get to this moment of transcendence, Disney's details work just below the surface to build a foundation for us to be immersed in the story—by inspiring our curiosity, providing knowledge, allowing us to search for and appreciate their beauty, and touching on our passion and purpose.

But it also happens most for me, my family, and many others, in one other location in Disney World. As we walk into...

...the *Plaza de los Amigos* marketplace inside the Mexico Pavilion at EPCOT. And, though it's technically inside, it doesn't feel that way. Instead, it looks and feels much more like what it's supposed to be. A small, colorful village marketplace under twilight skies...

...past an elegant, blue-lit tiled fountain, then through kiosks and wheeled carts selling crafts and other wares. With hanging lanterns crossing above, providing warm orange-yellow light against the blues and blacks of the "sky." A pyramid stands in the distance—across a dark, rippling lagoon—and deep in a jungle, with a slowly erupting volcano behind it...

...while far in the back and to the left is the entrance to the *Gran Fiesta Tour Starring the Three Caballeros* attraction, and skirting the lagoon is the *San Angel Inn Restaurante.* Finally, surrounding it all are village shops and homes, many with stairways and balconies decorated with flowers. And windows filled with Disney's famous flickering lights.

"When I was doing a small project in the Mexico Pavilion at EPCOT, I first went to Mexico and travelled from city to city experiencing different aspects of the country, including the sights, sounds, smells, tastes, and emotions of being there," recalled Steve Probus, former art director, set decorator principal, and field art director for Walt Disney Imagineering, and author of the upcoming book, *The Journey to Imagineering.*

"During that trip, the Mexican Tourism Office, which was involved with Disney on the development of that pavilion exhibit, would have representatives drop me off with a different local tourist official in each state I visited. I would then visit churches, shops, artists' studios, and art complexes, and even go to people's homes to see how the 'world of Mexico' could be translated to this small project in the pavilion. This represents the extent that Disney will go to—to create an environment and authentic details for the stories to come alive and be believable.

"On every stop, I would feel the pride that people in Mexico had for their country. I would sit in their homes and have tea with them. I would watch them work, oftentimes with old-fashioned tools. When I asked why they did what they did, they said they wanted to give something back to someone, and that in some cases their passions were fostered while passed down from generation to generation. They did not just do it to make money. They wanted to make a difference and bring joy to folks, just as Walt always wanted to do in his animation, films, and parks. I still cannot believe how humble the people were there.

"That trip is also why, when I go to EPCOT and step into the marketplace in the middle of the Mexico Pavilion, I feel like I'm right back in Mexico and all the places I visited there. Yes, it's romanticized, but with the smells, the sights, the sounds, and the people, it feels like I'm there. Immersed.

"Which also ties back to the main questions Joe Rohde, who I worked with, would always ask us about the attractions we were working on: 'Are you telling the story the right way? Are there any contradictions? Is there passion in it?'"

Yes, I swear there were times in the *Plaza de los Amigos* where, for just a moment or two, instead of thinking I was standing in a Disney building, I believed I was standing in a small Mexican village.

In those moments, I was fully immersed. Moments that happened "gradually, then suddenly." Where in one instance, it's one thing, and in the very next, it's something altogether different, and you don't even remember what came before. Those moments that come right after "Once upon a time..." if we trust the storyteller, and their storytelling is strong enough, that we take that step over the transom.

Theron's Keys #3: Pulling guests into the story

The marketplace in the Mexico Pavilion is a wonderful example of how Disney uses "visual hierarchy," or the arranging of design elements by their order of importance, in its storytelling to pull guests in—including in their parks and movies. The intent is to create a multi-dimensional image that the guest or viewer can travel through, like the effect accomplished with the multi-plane camera on *Snow White and the Seven Dwarfs*.

In this case, as a guest enters the marketplace under the *Plaza de los Amigos* sign, they immediately see the "establishing shot," which allows a view of the entire setting, the foreground, the mid-ground, and the background, all supported by angles, lighting, and other key elements to create a sense of place.

Next, the guest walks down the ramp past the fountain onto a cobblestone path and into the "medium close-up shot" of the story, with carts, pennants, smells, music, and native language being spoken, that fulfills their expectations of what it would be like to be in that place.

Then, they get to the "close-up shot" at the *San Angel Inn Restaurante*, where they're able to take in more of the details, and they meet—and speak with—all the Cast Members who are actually from Mexico, and taste the authentic food.

Each of the details at these various levels draws the guest into the reality of the scene and the experience, and each has to "pay off." Then, as they visit the Mexico Pavilion multiple times in the future, they can see things they've never seen before, which solidifies the experience for them and creates even more of that emotional connection.

The sorcerer is in the house

So, there I was, here we all are, in that moment right before falling asleep (or waking up, depending on how you look at it).

When a storyteller we trust becomes a sorcerer (apprentice included). Begins to weave their spell, using details as their incantation. A little more candy apple red here. The briny smell of ocean there. The rumbling sounds of distant thunder everywhere. Until they get it just right. When the spell works its way upon us, to the point where we don't remember ever meeting the sorcerer at all, and all we know is being alive, in the story.

Of course, sometimes the sorcerer is someone much closer to home.

My wife, for example, casts that same kind of spell whenever she prepares for guests to stay over at our house, and that preparation always starts with a list.

What's on the list? Cleaning projects, house projects (yes, we seem to always put an addition on our house to prepare for guests), grocery lists, special touches for our guests. Even elaborate meal menus if they're staying for a while. Something I like to call the "Gina Dining Plan (Florida Resident Prices Available)."

When I asked my wife why she is so intent on getting the details right for our guests, she said, "Because I want everything to be perfect. I want them to be pampered, to enjoy themselves. I don't want to miss any details or forget anything. A lot of times, for example, it's new things I want them to experience, like a recipe or a special smelling soap. Other times, it can just be something silly. Most of all, I just always want them to associate us and our house with the positive experiences they've had with staying over. I want to give them something they wouldn't get elsewhere, to feel special and at home."

Sound familiar? Paying attention to the details with such care that you actually create a new reality and invite others to enter it.

Yes, Disney's details do that, too, and, in the process, become a doorway to another world.

Where we, once again, feel like we're home.

DETAILS ARE THE DOORWAY

Questions

1. Is there a detail from a Disney attraction that most stands out for you? One that you can remember clearly to this day and love to share with others?

2. Did you ever look "to the right" on an attraction or resort when everyone else was "looking to the left," based on the design and flow of the attraction? If so, what did you see?

3. Have you had a *Plaza de los Amigos* moment with Disney, where you forgot where you were, and the imaginary became real?

4. How does it feel when you go somewhere, and you can tell they really planned for your arrival?

5. What might happen if, at home, you took a little longer to notice the details around you, both in the rooms and in the people?

4   Coming Home

"Because when I look at you, I can feel it. And I look at you and I'm home."

Dory to Marlin, *Finding Nemo*

O nce we've been immersed by the details, two words are typically all it takes.

"Welcome home."

If you're at a cocktail party and want to quickly figure out whether someone loves Disney or not, just share these two words along with your favorite Disney-related story.

Why?

Because doing so will typically get one of two reactions. A smile or an eye roll.

Why the smile? Well, that's easy. It means that, at one point in the past, they were possibly bitten by the Disney love bug (of course, we call him "Herbie"). And, because they were, those two words probably took them right back to that feeling. You know the one. That "weak in the knees, writing their name in your notebook, thinking the way they laugh is just the cutest" feeling of being in love. In this case, with Disney.

Ok, then, what about the people (and we know who you are!) who give the eye roll? Well, that's easy, too. It probably means they either a) don't love Disney, b) feel that the "Welcome home" phrase is overused, and possibly cheesy, or c) both of the above.

And I get it that some might not get it. At least at first.

After all, I don't believe I always loved Disney growing up. (And with that confession, a hush comes over the room, or at least, with you the reader, as you wonder how on Earth a guy who didn't love Disney ended up writing a book about how he, well, loves Disney.)

But wait, remember, I said I don't believe I *loved* Disney "growing up."

That's probably because, as a kid, I never saw most of the Disney classic animated movies, was too young to have grown up with the original version of *The Mickey Mouse Club*, and never went to Disney World or Disneyland on family vacations. Nope, the Wisconsin Dells was the pinnacle experience of my childhood travel experience.

But I did *like* Disney a whole bunch.

Wait, what?! You don't know what the Wisconsin Dells is? Well, first, it's in Wisconsin. (That part you probably got right away.) As for the rest, well, let's allow TripAdvisor.com to fill us in: "Shaped by the currents and curves of the Wisconsin River, the Wisconsin Dells has been a favorite family vacation destination for more than 150 years. An explosion of indoor water parks has turned the Dells from a summer hot spot to a year-round destination. Kids will enjoy the seemingly endless supply of fun and games, from go-karts to miniature golf, sideshows to thrill rides. If the weather's right, you can take a Duck tour of land and water and top it all off with a heaping helping of the local fudge." And, no, I don't get a commission if you go to the Wisconsin Dells. But if you do go, please send me some of that fudge!

That's because Disney was still a big part of my childhood. As mentioned in Chapter One, as a kid of the late 60s (as in 1960, not 1860—be nice), like many, I enjoyed watching *The Wonderful World of Disney* on TV on Sunday nights, knowing that when Tinker Bell sprinkled her pixie dust across the screen something magical was about to happen. And though I likely wouldn't have been able to put it into words then, I'm sure I felt that, for the rest of the show, I wouldn't have a care in the world.

Yes, some might say, "What 'cares' could a child have who is growing up in a pretty reasonable way?" Well, though to adults the thought of having a math test on Monday and not knowing who you're going to sit with at lunch might seem like a small concern, that's like an adult knowing they have to defend their departmental budget at work on Monday morning while also being concerned about a "clear the air" conversation they have to have with a colleague later in the week. And that's why children sometimes need a Disney escape as much, if not more, than we adults do.

I also liked the non-animated Disney movies, like the *Herbie the Love Bug* series, and Kurt Russell's Disney movies, like *The Computer Wore Tennis Shoes.*

But, like I said, I liked Disney.

Checking back with D23.com, we read that, "At 15, Kurt Russell was cast in his first Disney picture, *Follow Me, Boys!*, starring fellow Disney Legend Fred MacMurray. Walt Disney took an instant liking to Kurt and signed him to an exclusive Studio contract, making him the Studio's teen star of the 1960s and 70s...In the 1968 Disney musical *The One and Only, Genuine Original Family Band*, Kurt met a young dancer named Goldie Hawn; she would later become his real-life leading lady." Since then, of course, Kurt has been in other Disney movies, including *Miracle*, *Sky High*, and *Guardians of the Galaxy, Vol. 2*.

So, to be fair to the eye roller, if I was still in that "liking but not loving" Disney space, and in that space, as an adult, I went to any of the Disney parks or venues, or took a Disney Cruise, and a Cast Member greeted me with a "Welcome home," I'm guessing I might just roll my eyes, thinking it was a bit over the top.

Yes, I would understand—if I were still in like-mode.

But being who I am now, a grown man fully committed to Disney (yes, we even have promise rings), those two words have a much different effect.

As they do for many.

"Welcome home."

And as we've said, the feeling I get from those two words starts with the base of the pyramid. Yep, *that* pyramid. Our good friend Maslow's. With things like food, water, clothing, a place to lay our head in a way that's safe. And a feeling that when we're there, we belong.

In other words, the home we had as a child...or the one we always wanted.

But, before we move on to talking about how "Welcome home" actually feels on a Disney visit, let's do as our famous nanny friend, Julie Andrews, instructed in the not-originally-a-Disney-movie-but-is-now-one *The Sound of Music* and "...start at the very beginning, a very good place to start..."

The Sound of Music wasn't originally a Disney movie but became one. Huh? How? Well, though originally produced by 20th Century Fox, the Disney Studios acquired the rights to the film when it bought 21st Century Fox (yep, name change) in 2017. And, according to my painstaking research (an exhaustive Google search of about 14 minutes), I learned that the director of *The Sound of Music*, Robert Wise, selected Julie Andrews to play the role of Maria von Trapp in his film after seeing preview footage of her in *Mary Poppins* at the Disney Studios. See, all roads really do lead back to Disney.

And once again, I learned that there really is something to that "Disney feeling." Just like with *Chitty Chitty Bang Bang*, as discussed in Chapter One, if it feels a lot like a Disney movie, then it probably has connections to Disney. Just like if it looks, swims, and quacks like a duck, then it probably is one. Likely going by the name of Donald.

Which is to answer the question, "What is home?" Because to really understand if Disney feels like one, we must first know how one is supposed to feel.

"I have so many memories of watching Walt on Sunday night TV," says long-time Disney fan Hank Reed. "Fast forward, and I remember taking our young kids to Disney World. On that first trip, we got autographs from the Seven Dwarfs, then stepped out of line to sit in the shade for a few minutes.

"While we did, Esmerelda came out and spent about fifteen minutes focused just on my daughter. We also ran into her again before we left. A bit of magic must have happened in those moments because, afterwards, my daughter said she wanted to come back and work at Disney.

"Fast forward another twenty years and my daughter was working at Disney World! When we visited her, we met many of her co-workers and leaders and you could tell she was home.

"I am a bit older and more sentimental than a lot of folks, but I do know this—if you find a kid's passion and encourage it a bit, it just may turn out to be something. And those old memories of Uncle Walt's Sunday night talks, they live on. Blessings, ya'll."

What is home?

Of course, that question deserves a book of its own. And actually that book, those books, have been written. As have poems. And plays. And songs. And dances. And paintings... and, well, pretty much every art form.

"Well, what about movies?" I hear you ask.

My answer, "Oh, Auntie Em, there's no place like (I'll let you fill in the blank)!"

Looking at all the different ways humans have defined "home," it seems to come down to the fact that, yes, home is a place, but even more, a feeling. One that I feel—and likely millions, if not billions, of others around the world, including you, presumably—with Disney.

In fact, I believe that's why so many people use the phrase "second home" when talking about a Disney park or other Disney location.

Now, please don't misunderstand me. By calling Disney a home, or even, at a minimum, a "second home," I'm not naïve enough to believe that Disney can completely make up for things done or missed in childhood. That would be ludicrous. But, for many, I believe it can give them some of it.

In fact, it doesn't take a psychologist, a Disney historian, or even another one of my famous overly exhausting research sessions on Google to assume that Walt reimagined parts of his childhood with Disneyland, both the childhood that was and the one he would have wanted.

That is the power of "Welcome home." To time travel, go back in time, if you will, and reset.

A reset that happened for me, my wife, and our children every time we got off the Magical Express bus, walked into whatever Disney World resort we were staying at (most often the Beach Club), and heard "Welcome home" for the first time that trip. When we did, we automatically knew what was going to happen:

First, that we didn't have to worry about food, clothing, or shelter for our entire stay (remember Chapter One?).

Second, we knew that we were in a place that felt safe (heck, we felt safe enough as parents to nap while on certain attractions, like *Carousel of Progress* and the former *Universe of Energy*). Of course, that feeling of safety can be a double-edged sword, where people feel like Disney's "got it covered" so they don't need to worry about safety too much.

Third, we knew that we felt like we belonged, surrounded by strangers who immediately became friends—guests and Cast Members alike. Now, were they really friends? (Of course not, though some could be by the end of the trip.) But that last sentence was the analytical me talking. And the analytical me wasn't allowed on Disney vacations often. I'd usually leave him at home, streaming classic *Honeymooners* episodes while eating Doritos, unless he stowed away in my carry-on...which happened a few times. It wasn't pretty.

Yep, food, clothing, shelter, safety, and belonging.

That's how you spell "home."

One of the most powerful feelings we humans can have.

So, though some may say Disney's "Welcome home" is cheesy, for those who do believe, it means a lot. Especially in the tough moments, like when a loved one who used to experience a Disney park or cruise with you is gone. Sometimes it's the little places or times that otherwise mean nothing in particular to others, like the breezeway under *Spaceship Earth*, that become a place to reconnect with them.

And why Disney will always be home.

"A lot of people, including myself, call Disney World 'home,'" says Kathleen Logan Wolfe, founder of Get Down to Disness. "But it wasn't until recently that I really understood what that meant.

"To me, home was always my parent's house. There was nothing like it, both as a kid and adult. Now, let me first say, we weren't rich, not by any stretch. But when we took a couple of trips to Disney World as kids, we were allowed to basically have whatever we wanted—including having ice cream for dinner!

"It was a fantastic place to have fun. And because my parents had never gone there before they had kids, we were able to experience it new together.

"Growing up, too, my mom and I loved sharing our Disney passion. We would always chat about what was new, the latest tips—everything!

"I couldn't get enough.

"Then, about eight years ago, as we were planning to go to Disney World to celebrate our parents' 50th wedding anniversary, my mother unexpectedly passed away. But because my father knew the last thing she would want to do was be the reason we cancelled a Disney trip, we still went.

"That trip was beautiful...and awful.

"Because around every corner, there was a memory of my mom waiting for me. Not just on the attractions, but in the 'in between' places, like benches and the breezeway underneath *Spaceship Earth*. I even felt her memory at *Chef Mickey's*.

"So, it was on that trip that it really hit me how much Disney had become our second home. Obviously, childhood homes are important, but we leave them, they get sold, and so on. But Disney was always there growing up. And now with the huge void left by my mom's passing, it's often where I feel closest to her.

"You know, I always tried to put my feelings about Disney into words, but I never quite could. But whenever I go on *Carousel of Progress* now, I always leave an empty seat next to me for my mom and imagine her there, clapping, laughing, and singing along to 'There's a Great Big Beautiful Tomorrow.'

"And that moment, for me, now says it all."

"My main interest as a child was Disney," says Aydin Turgay, founder of the Theme ParkLife Facebook fan page. "I would go to Disney World with my mom every spring break. Then came EPCOT. And I was really sucked in! I loved how she and I could walk around the park and experience futurism and countries around the World Showcase, including their culture and food, which inspired me to learn more about cooking.

"Around high school, sadly, my parents split up, and she moved back to Turkey. At the time, since my dad and I hadn't been on trips together, he was looking to bond with me—not easy to do with a teenager! So he said, 'Why don't we go to Disney World, just like you used to with your mom?' He bought a *Birnbaum Walt Disney World Resort* travel guide and said, 'You choose what you want to do. You plan it. Whatever you want.' So I handled all of that, including the dining reservations, which was very cool because The Food Network had just launched, and I was fascinated with food trends and chefs.

"We had a great trip! I remember having excellent meals, like Carne Asada at *San Angel Inn Restaurante* in the Mexico Pavilion at EPCOT, and another one at *Fulton's Crab House* (now *Paddlefish*) in Downtown Disney (now Disney Springs). We loved seafood, so we got King Crab legs. I remember putting them next to our faces and us laughing as we took pictures! That trip was amazing and gave me so many special memories, memories that became even more special when my dad died suddenly about twelve years ago.

"At the time he died, my fiancé and I were planning a destination wedding for the coming year. But, seeing what I was going through, she said, 'You know, you told me about this amazing trip you had with your dad, so what if we do an early honeymoon, stay at the same hotel, and eat the same meals you ate, everything?'

"So, we did.

"During the trip, I asked my fiancé to take a picture of me in the breezeway under *Spaceship Earth* because on that earlier trip with my dad, we'd taken a picture in that same spot. And when she did, I truly realized the power of the Disney parks.

"Because, even when I was a kid we never lived in the same place for long. We moved every five years or so. So I don't really have one place to go back to—to remember all the happy memories from my childhood. But after my fiancé took that picture, it occurred to me that I would always have Disney World. A place where, no matter what, I can relive the memories with my mom and dad, my sister, even early ones with my grandmother. And I would always have a place where I can create new memories with my own family, where I can keep going back. It will always be there."

Are you convinced yet that Disney is like home for many of us? (Though if you bought this book, borrowed it from a friend, or checked it out of a library, I'm guessing it shouldn't take too much convincing?)

If not, let's try an experiment.

The experiment

Ok, close your eyes (unless you're driving, or otherwise operating heavy machinery—so I'm guessing "light machinery" might still be an open question).

Now imagine what the ideal home would look and feel like for you. Warm and cozy? Comfort food on the table? Music playing in the background—or possibly the TV? Favorite drinks in the fridge and snacks in the pantry? Comfortable chairs and couch to sit on? Nice soft or hard bed (depending how you like it) to sleep on? Extra blanket on that bed in the winter, or window in the bedroom slightly open in the summer with a fan going overhead? Closet full of clothes for every season? A fireplace to read by and a lake to stroll by? And what about a tree swing, freshly cut grass, and badminton net?

Next, envision what it would feel like as soon as you walked through the front door of that imaginary home. Would you be welcomed warmly? Surrounded by people who share your history, know your dreams, and were counting the minutes until you arrived?

Ok, now the big question, wait for it...

How would you *feel* there?

Pause.

No, really, I know it's tough in this "got to get things done so I can get on to the next thing" world, but pause for just a second and...let...that...feeling...sink...in.

Great, now that it has, remember it as we think back to...

...that moment of walking into a Disney resort and hearing "Welcome home," or boarding a Disney cruise ship as they welcome your family by name.

Yes, that's it. The same feeling.

And really, is there anything better than being welcomed back to the place you love, knowing that for a while at least, at Disney specifically, the only thing you're going to have to worry about is whether you want a Dole Whip or Mickey Bar? (And yes, I do hear some of you yelling "Churro!" there in the back?)

That's why a Disney "Welcome home" immediately takes me back, as it does for so many, no matter whether it's their first time or if they've been going so long that they already know where most of the Hidden Mickeys are.

Hidden Mickeys...ok, ok, don't get me started. Ask 100 people about the definition of a "Hidden Mickey" and you'll get 172 different answers. So, here's my take on them: they're hidden (or not—so—hidden) images of Mickey Mouse's head and ears intentionally designed into a Disney attraction or other structure or venue. To learn more about them and join the obsession, go to hiddenmickeyguy.com or just Google "Hidden Mickeys."

Who's this Hidden Mickey Guy we speak of? Well, it's Steve Barrett (who contributed a story for this book, and is another of those great, kind people I've met on this journey). But please, when you and your friends argue about whether a Mickey is hidden, please don't call me to settle it. I have a dental appointment that day.

Now of course, I get it that Cast Members are trained to say it and they have to probably say it over a hundred (thousand?) times a day. But all those years when I, my wife, or our kids would hear it, I guarantee we weren't thinking, "Geez, that's cheesy."

Why?

Well, it's a combination of two things—what I bring *with* me and what is waiting *for* me.

What I bring with me is the expectation of fun, relaxation, and letting go. I bring the memories from the many times in the past that I have visited, along with all the Disney experiences I've had in between those visits. I bring with me my wife and my kids, who each have their own Disney memories.

And what is waiting for me? Adventure. New memories. Seeing Disney through the eyes of our new granddaughter, just as we once saw it new through the eyes of our children.

Really, in all, "Welcome home" for me is just another way of saying "Once upon a time." It signals a beginning, an invitation into a new story that's also connected to past ones.

Theron's Keys #4: Homecoming

As Imagineers, we think about the total journey of our guests and every touchpoint along that journey. That's why, for example, when you boarded the Magical Express bus at the Orlando airport, it wasn't like a parade float with stuff moving and people dancing in the aisles. That would be too much. We had to remember that it was a transition from the guests' real world to Disney World, or their "second home," as you often hear them say.

In a sense, then, the Magical Express just had to be efficient, have good air conditioning, a driver with great customer service, and a wonderful welcome video. It was then the perfect first chapter in the story of their visit. And that applies to however the guests would experience their own unique entry into Disney's "world."

As we know, from that first moment, that story then needs to make an emotional connection with the guests, leveraging their five senses, which then helps them build memories. Then, when you have memories that have an emotional component and you're attached to that memory in a positive way, it makes them even more powerful and enduring. And of course, they fuel endorphins, ultimately making it a happy place for you. One that feels like home.

The last word on the subject?

Well, that comes from *How Does Disney Do That?* Facebook group contributor Daniel Moorefield, who said, "What does Disney mean to me? For me, that it's always been there. Seeing that castle down Main Street, exploring lands in the Magic Kingdom, going to EPCOT and being in Future World. I can't put it into words. Nothing more I can really say. It's another home for me."

Thanks, Dan. And of course, after we've been invited into the story by a storyteller we trust, and the details have immersed us enough to feel like we're home, what's next?

To grow up, of course. Before we grow back down.

Questions

1. What is "home" to you?

2. What do you feel when you hear "Welcome home"?

3. Does Disney feel like a second home to you? If so, why?

4. Is there a specific Disney movie, park, or cruise moment that you can recall when you thought of Disney being home?

5. Do you think that, if you visited any Disney park around the world that you haven't yet visited, went on a Disney cruise you haven't been on, etc., you'd also feel that "home" feeling?

5

Growing Up and Growing Back Down Again

"Why do we have to grow up? I know more adults who have the children's approach to life...They are not afraid to be delighted with simple pleasures, and they have a degree of contentment with what life has brought..."

Walt Disney

T
o prepare for writing this chapter, I did what any normal writer would do.

Watched home movies.

Though, to clarify, they'd really be called "second home" movies, because they were from past trips with our kids to our second home, Disney World. And, to clarify even further, I watched them with my wife.

However, to clarify my clarifications above, before we even got to watching them, we had to figure out if our old technology would work with our new technology. Namely, would our DVD player (which hardly anyone has anymore) even recognize the small discs from our old video camera (which no one has anymore) and would our VHS player (yes, I see you all out there laughing at me and I'm taking names) recognize the small tapes (yes, actual tapes) from our still even older video camera?

Once we wrestled the technology into submission, we then had to deal with four different remotes so...

...12 hours later, we finally started watching. And you would think, with all that time to prepare, we'd be ready emotionally for what happened next.

We weren't.

Meaning, originally we thought we were sitting down to watch old Disney trip videos so I could gather stories for this chapter. But what my wife and I both ended up with were lumps in our throats and the need to buy more Kleenex.

That's because for the next several hours we saw our kids, Jeremy, Matthew, and Alexandra, literally grow up before our eyes, with Disney as the background. And watching them change—their faces, bodies, clothes, mannerisms, the phrases they used, all of it—was quite something.

Another gift from Disney to us. Unwrapped, unannounced, and straight to the heart.

Growing up with Disney

There was Jeremy, our oldest, "pre-teenish" at the time of the first movie, providing Spielberg-like directorial "guidance" to me as I filmed his younger brother Matthew, five years younger, and sister Alexandra, eight years younger.

We watched as he seemingly realized that writing was more my thing; he proceeded to gently remove the video camera from my hand and began calmly capturing his siblings as they went on attractions. At the same time, he also ably fulfilled his big brother role by encouraging his siblings throughout the day—helping Matthew locate attractions on the park maps while gently nudging Alexandra to try the splash pad near *Mission: SPACE* at EPCOT.

Later that evening, while watching another "second home" movie, we saw Jeremy scuba-diving in the giant aquarium in The Living Seas (now The Seas with Nemo & Friends) as part of the EPCOT DiveQuest experience. It took me back to our being there—watching him in that moment, waving to Matthew on the other side of the glass and reading the notes

Alexandra was writing for him on a pad of paper, all while surrounded by 5.7 million gallons of water and over 5,500 sea creatures. And he didn't miss a beat. Or a breath.

Next up in the movies was Matthew, who from an early age could decipher and draw any map. At the beginning of each of our Disney trips, this "child cartographer" would walk up to the maps display rack in our resort, grab one for each park, and begin his reconnaissance.

Later, as we'd enter the first park, he'd immediately transform into our intrepid guide, hacking away at any navigational confusion with his machete-like mind (and, yes, that was a terribly tortured metaphor, but no metaphors were actually harmed in the making of this book).

As we made our way through the park, he'd confidently walk in front, letting us know where we were and what was coming up, along with features of the attractions we were passing, sprinkled in here and there with some historical facts about the park. As he did, he seemed to almost be walking *in* the map.

Most important, as Matthew shepherded us we'd regularly mention how amazed we were by his ability to guide us. When we did, I swear his chest puffed out a bit.

It was a confidence he also showed when conducting exhaustive searches for Hidden Mickeys using Steve Barrett's instantly recognizable *Hidden Mickeys Field Guide* series of books (which he'd hold up in front of him just like the map) along with going on even the most challenging rides as soon as he was tall enough to ride. And I do mean "as soon," like five minutes.

Rides like *Expedition Everest, Tower of Terror,* and *Rock 'n' Roller Coaster Starring Aerosmith.* A daring approach that foreshadowed the fact that, as of today, he's ridden many of the tallest, fastest coasters in the world...about 14,003 times by my count.

Then, of course, there was our little girl, Alexandra. As Gina and I watched the next home movie, we saw ourselves with the kids having breakfast at *Cinderella's Royal Table* in Cinderella Castle in the Magic Kingdom.

As each princess came up to meet our daughter, she would smile, quietly talk with them, and then confidently pose for a picture. Of course, when the princesses came up, they didn't just say "Hi!," sign her autograph book, and walk over to the next child. No, they did what Disney Cast Members do while representing the characters. They took time. And they were kind.

And as they talked with her, her eyes brightened. Very subtle, but if I could have imagined what she was thinking, it would have been, "All of these princesses came to meet me!"

On to the next movie, where Alexandra danced and sang in front of our bleachers at the *Fantasmic* pre-show at Disney-MGM Studios (now Disney's Hollywood Studios). As Jeremy filmed her (he had signed a multi-picture deal by this point), she performed for everyone around us, giving it her all, and by their applause and laughter you would have thought *she* was the show.

In another movie we saw Alexandra dance next to the belly

dancer who was part of the Mo'Rockin band at the Morocco Pavilion in EPCOT. As she did, she'd glance at the belly dancer and copy her moves almost perfectly. The crowd loved it, and so did the belly dancer. Oh, and by the way, Mo'Rockin did indeed rock more!

Alexandra's ability to put on an energetic show at *Fantasmic* and with Mo'Rockin foreshadowed her ability to get Taylor Swift's attention at a concert years later in Milwaukee. With Taylor's favorite number (13) and lyrics written in color on Alexandra's face and arms, and dancing with that same passion in the aisle, our daughter drew Taylor's attention from where she stood up above, singing "Love Story" from a mechanized "balcony" traveling over the crowd. Once Taylor saw Alexandra, she pointed out my daughter to her crew. That meant that Alexandra, her cousin Gaby, Gina, my sister Bobbie, and my mother-in-law June ended up backstage after the show at one of Taylor's famous "T Parties" for fans.

To this day, whenever someone sees the picture of Taylor with all of them, I can tell they want to ask if it's fake. It's not. Though my picture on the shelf next to it golfing with Ernest Hemingway may have been touched up a bit.

As the night ended and Gina and I packed up the movies, we talked about how great it was to watch our kids growing up in one night, and at the place we all loved.

For that, I don't have words.

Well, maybe one.

Wonder.

And that's just our experience. Think of the millions upon millions of parents who have seen their millions upon millions of children all become the center of attention at a Disney park, resort, cruise, or other location or event, and who have also seen their children, in those places, show their strengths and accomplish things they didn't think they could. Whether it was getting the high score on *Buzz Lightyear's Space Ranger Spin* attraction, deciding to overcome their fear of riding *Space Mountain*, or feeling a burst of pride when asked to lead a Disney parade or take part in an ensemble at Disney World, like Rob Walter's daughters.

"I remember several distinct Disney memories with my daughters," said Rob Walter, Disney fan and a senior clinical data analyst.

"One was about 17 years ago, when my former wife and I were with our oldest daughter, Kelsey, who was about 4. We were sitting on a curb on the side of Main Street at the Magic Kingdom, waiting for the nighttime parade, while Kelsey danced around waving a light-up wand. As she did, a Cast Member asked if we thought she would be interested in leading the parade. We immediately said 'Yes!' So, he then explained to Kelsey what she would need to do. After that, as her mom remembers, they announced to the crowd that 'Grand Marshal Kelsey' would be leading the parade, and Kelsey was so excited.

"The other wonderful moments were when our younger daughter, Hailey, went on two Disney World field trips with her middle school and high school orchestras (I chaperoned both). The best part was the opportunity for the students to professionally record their ensemble and then see it set to Disney film footage!

"Most of all, today, as I remember Kelsey being in that parade and Hailey taking part in those ensembles, I remember how proud I was of them then, and still am. It was so special to have that happening—and in a place that I had been going to since childhood."

So, whether it's Rob's children, the children of all those other millions upon millions of parents, or our own, Disney gives them all the opportunity to become the heroes of their own stories as they grow up. As it did with Jeremy becoming a young filmmaker, a scuba diver in one of the world's biggest aquariums, and an encouraging big brother. Matthew navigating the parks and meeting the challenge of every Hidden Mickey and rollercoaster he meets. Alexandra realizing that she's well worth a visit by the Disney princesses and putting on her own oh-so-popular shows.

> In growing up, we see how Maslow's pyramid continues to apply, as children feel comfortable enough at Disney to learn, play, explore, and create, which can make them more confident and help them find their path.

The path is set

And with so many of these childhood Disney experiences, they don't just matter in the moment, they matter for the future, and for the careers and paths that children take. As they did from up above for Jim VanOstenbridge.

"Jim VanOstenbridge, board member for The Carolwood Society, photographer, and solution architect.

"My story started like many others, as a child watching *The Wonderful World of Disney* on Sunday nights and then my family's first trip to Walt Disney World. At the Magic Kingdom, my parents ushered me into a pirate ship on *Peter Pan's Flight* where I would experience a perspective that would shape my life and career: flying over London. At that moment it seemed more real than real. Ever since, I appreciated every opportunity to see the world from above, and today I help organizations apply geography—which includes the use of satellite, aerial, and drone imagery—to work together in new and remarkable ways. I also have since become a professional photographer, focusing much of my time on Disney, its trains, parks, and so on.

"None of this would have continued without my wife finding her inspirations as well. After we met in college, she and I went to Disney World. As we boarded the Doom Buggies of the *Haunted Mansion*, she realized they connected to the board game she had played when she was young called 'The Haunted Mansion.' All those memories came rushing back to her as we traversed the scenes of Happy Haunts, and she found her connection with the place.

"It has also been so special to meet Imagineers like Kevin Rafferty, Tony Baxter, Bob Gurr, and others. It never disappoints because, when you meet them, you immediately see how the Disney journey has been crafted, how they were able to take an idea, bat it around, and make it real enough that it creates an amazing experience for fans.

"That resonates with me because I also believe in creating things or guiding people into creating things that will change the world for the better. And that's what the people at Disney do—bring together engineering and emotion."

Theron's Keys #5: Becoming the hero

Disney gives us all the chance to become the hero of our own story. When you think of Jim VanOstenbridge, whose story we just heard, look at everything that happened on *Peter Pan's Flight* that helped him become who he is.

Maybe he saw Disney's *Peter Pan* movie before he rode the attraction, so he had a connection with the story. Maybe he wanted to be a "lost boy." And maybe he remembered how the movie came to life for him on the attraction as he "flew" over London. In a way, that moment burned the memory into his brain and created a lifelong emotional connection.

And, as he says in his story, he was transformed by that experience to the point where it informed what he wanted to be. Because, in a sense, in that ship over London he may have decided that he wanted to create that experience for others, to help them see the world as he saw it in that moment. Which then resulted in him choosing a career, and finding real accomplishment, in a field that helps people see the world from up above.

Plus, he took that emotional connection with Disney and translated it into his love of photography, especially of Disney. Then, as he relates that story now as an adult, I'm guessing he "becomes" that boy again for a few moments.

In fact, it reminds me of being a boy myself, sitting in a theater in 1977, watching *Star Wars* (now part of Disney, of course, and then only called *Star Wars*) and realizing that was what I wanted to do. Create other worlds and bring people into them, help them step through a picture frame into the picture. I grew up to do that, to immerse people in experiences, especially at theme parks. And by doing that, like Jim, I took something that transformed me and used it to hopefully transform others. And of course, when I do those things, it takes me right back to being that boy again, sitting in that theater.

Of course, because Imagineers and so many others at Disney typically start out as fans, they can usually trace their love of Disney back to their childhoods, too. And then they can often draw a line from those childhood experiences to what they wanted to do, and many times did, with their lives.

Speaking of drawing, that was a big part of the seemingly straight line that led former Imagineer Joe Lanzisero to his role with Disney, along with some surprising classmates along the way (including a very surprising Best Man at his wedding).

"I was born the year after Disneyland opened," states Joe Lanzisero, former senior vice president, Walt Disney Imagineering, and current executive vice president and senior art director, Zeitgeist Design + Production.

"Growing up, I remember watching 'Uncle Walt' every Sunday night on TV. I also loved to draw as a child and that stuck with me. So, watching Disney on those Sunday nights really captured my imagination to the point where, even as a kid, I knew I wanted to work for Disney someday.

"So, it's not surprising that I ended up going to school at CalArts (California Institute of the Arts) in their Character Animation program, starting in 1975. In fact, my first class included several students who would become famous, including John Lasseter (*Toy Story, A Bug's Life, Cars*), John Musker (*The Little Mermaid, Aladdin*), Brad Bird (*The Incredibles, Ratatouille*), and Tim Burton (*The Nightmare Before Christmas, James and the Giant Peach*). On a side note, Tim and I carpooled up to CalArts and he was the best man at my wedding!

"At CalArts, we were basically a bunch of young kids who loved to draw, loved storytelling, and loved the emotion that people at Disney put into what they did. So, you can imagine how excited I was when I was hired by Disney into their Animation Department as a feature animator.

"Then, after learning about Walt Disney Imagineering, I moved over there and took on design roles, including on Disney's Typhoon Lagoon Water Park at Disney World and *Phantom Manor* at Disneyland Paris. And in the early 90s, they gave this young waif an opportunity to oversee an entire land celebrating the original 'Fab 5' plus Roger Rabbit—Mickey's Toontown!

"I was given the opportunity to lead the concept, design, and production of two new Disney cruise ships—the *Dream* and the *Fantasy*. And I worked on many other projects, including the *Fantasia Gardens* and *Winter Summerland* miniature golf courses at Walt Disney World, Tokyo DisneySea, and Tokyo Disneyland.

"I also oversaw design on Hong Kong Disneyland as we added three new lands to the park. In fact, the attraction I'm most proud of is the *Mystic Manor* dark ride. When people walked out, we wanted them to feel real empathy for Lord Henry Mystic's pet monkey. And we also wanted guests to leave saying, 'How does Disney do that?'"

Of course, sometimes, that line drawn from childhood can only be seen as straight in retrospect, as it was with Colette Piceau, who after starting out in acting, "discovered" a strength she already somehow knew she had.

"As a child, I loved the stories I heard in the Disney records that came with picture books. They were a big part of my growing up," said Colette Piceau, independent writer, Walt Disney Imagineering, and current head writer/creative director for It Ain't Shakespeare.

"After graduating college, I lived in New York as a professional actress with my husband at that time who was also an actor. Fortunately, a friend at Disney World helped us get auditions there. After we were selected, my first role was in the *Hoop-De-Doo Musical Revue* at Disney's Fort Wilderness Resort.

"I then got a role in the *Indiana Jones Epic Stunt Spectacular* at Disney-MGM Studios. Prior to its opening in 1989, the show's producers asked the actors if we had a cool idea for the pre-show. Luckily, I did! So I quickly wrote it, rehearsed it with my husband, and we performed it for the producers. They liked it, so it became the original pre-show. After that, I was invited to join other brainstorming sessions and writing projects, including writing for the Disney Cruise Line and the *Adventurers Club* nightclub on Pleasure Island.

"Looking back, I'm not quite sure what gave me the courage to write that first pre-show. I didn't really consider myself a writer at the time and hadn't even studied writing. However, I did know I was a storyteller. It came easy to me. So, finding out that I could also write was a real gift in my life. Something I discovered in myself that had always been there—which, of course, sounds like the theme of many Disney stories, too.

"As both a performer and writer, I was always thinking about how I wanted the audience to feel. I wanted to connect with them at an emotional level, from the heart, to get them involved and connected. Because the audience won't care unless they feel connected. And they definitely won't feel wonder until they feel that way, too.

"As part of that connection, the audience members would feed off each other's energy and that of the performers. After all, in all human beings, there is an ancient link to storytelling in the biology of our brains. When we're all together, and there's a story being told, we connect with others. Then, when we connect with them, we feel their energy. And when we feel their energy, we feel our own, too."

Sometimes, also, a child's future can be changed just by receiving a Disney book (no, I don't mean this one, though now that you mention it...), as happened when former Imagineer Brian Collins' parents bought him a book as a child that literally changed his life. And, as you read it, really begin to notice how important the role of the encouraging parent or mentor is in so many of these stories. Surprising? Not really. But it's good every now and then to be amazed even by unsurprising things.

"When I was young, my parents brought home a souvenir book for me that promoted the coming Walt Disney World Resort," said Brian Collins, former Walt Disney Imagineer, and current global innovation consultant and founder of The Brainstorm Institute. "That book, which I still have, included fascinating behind-the-scenes photos. It really captured my imagination, and what kid wouldn't think, 'How cool would it be to work at that place when I grow up?'

"Years later, after working as a scriptwriter and video producer out of college, I moved to Orlando and applied to Disney since they were building the Disney-MGM Studios park (now Disney's Hollywood Studios). While I hoped to put my production experience to work right away, my first job was checking in guests at the front desk of Disney's Contemporary Resort.

"But then one day, while in line for a Cast Member preview of *The Great Movie Ride* at the soon-to-be-opened Studios, I chatted with a production assistant who helped coordinate the park's then-active film and TV production schedule. We hit it off, and soon afterward I was assisting on the backlot and soundstages.

"From that point, I got to work on the grand openings of several major attractions and expansions like *Star Tours*, *Wonders of Life*, Disney's Yacht and Beach Club, Pleasure Island, *Splash Mountain*, and the grand opening of the Studios itself!

"All this experience led me to Walt Disney Imagineering where I was brought on as a show writer, crafting scripts and other spiels, including the reimagining of the *Jungle Cruise* queue. Of course, this was all amazing to me because I was always in awe of the Imagineers and had always thought working for WDI was out of reach...a 'moonshot' if you will.

"Coincidentally, one of my largest projects as an Imagineer was getting to 'plus' or enhance *The Great Movie Ride*. That was particularly special after having been an anonymous test rider just a year or so before.

"Looking back, a few 'Wow!' moments really stand out for me from working at Disney. The first was when I received my first Disney name tag during onboarding. That was then surpassed a few years later when I was handed my WDI name tag.

"Another 'Wow!' moment, or I should say 'moments,' occurred whenever I had the chance to go into the parks and silently witness the guests enjoying the scripts, spiels, and attractions I worked on. How could you not be humbled by seeing the smiles on their faces?

"Finally, of course, some of the most memorable times at WDI were having the chance to meet Disney Imagineering Legends like Marc Davis and his wife Alice, Rolly Crump, and one of my favorites, John Hench. All of these were people who worked closely with Walt to bring his ideas to life!

"Being an Imagineer was an honor and something I never took lightly, and still don't to this day."

At other times, a child's unique way of seeing the world can be ignited by details at Disney that we might not have even realized a child would notice, as they did with Dave Yost. As you read his story, just imagine a child thinking about how Disney does inventory—that is what's so cool about kids, that each child brings their own unique perspective and passion to the world.

"As far back as I can remember," said Dave Yost, long-time Disney fan, "I've liked Disney for its operational aspects. Of course, most kids like it for the characters, the rides, and so on, but I was wowed by its operations and the planning behind it all.

"For example, I always loved the landscaping and architecture at Disney World. There was also something whimsical about both, and about how Disney kept everything so neat and trimmed. EPCOT really thrilled me, too—at one point, you drive *under* a water canal!

"Yes, I was a kid, but somehow I just knew that Disney ran different. I was fascinated by all of it, the utilidors under Magic Kingdom, how they staffed their front desks at the resorts to keep the lines almost nonexistent, the timing of the ferry boats to the Magic Kingdom, how they handled the ride queues to optimize how many people could get on the rides and how long it took to wait, how people were constantly filling inventory in the stores to keep the shelves full, and so on.

"If I were to have a reset button, I'd become an architectural engineer for Disney. That would also give me the chance to go back to that feeling I had as a kid again. Why would I want to work there? To make everyone as happy as possible."

Yes, not surprisingly, different aspects of Disney inspire children in different ways. For some it's the parks and their operations, for others it's the TV shows or songs, and for still others, the animation itself is key, as it was for Disney historian and author Didier Ghez, along with the inspiration to travel the world.

"I was always fascinated by Disney and that fascination has evolved," said Didier Ghez, Disney historian, vice president at Starz, and author of the *They Drew As They Pleased* series, the *Walt's People* series, and *The Origins of Walt Disney's True-Life Adventures*.

"As a child, I had my first real exposure to Disney by reading *Mickey Mouse Magazine*, the way many kids in Europe learned about Disney. In the magazine, I also saw Donald Duck and Scrooge McDuck discover the world, which made me want to.

"Next, my parents took me to the cinema to see Disney movies, starting with *Pinocchio*, and they brought the movies home, too. Watching them, I noticed there was something special about the stories and characters, and definitely the animation. In fact, it was the movies that really got me interested in Disney animation.

"One of the moments I most remember was before my family took our first vacation to Disney World in 1972. I remember obsessing about going, seeing the park call out to me from the covers of *Life* and *Look* magazines. In fact, I even made a list of the attractions I most wanted to go on.

"Afterwards, as I became a teenager and continued to watch the movies and be exposed to more of Disney, I really began to understand how extremely talented their artists were. So, I wanted to learn everything I could about them. And the more I found out, the more fascinated I got. That then led to me writing about Disney, Walt, his animators, and more. And that fascination has just continued to grow. In fact, I'm sure it will be a life-long passion."

For Stephanie and Danny Shuster, co-founders of *WDW Magazine*, *DLR Magazine*, and the *DCL Magazine Blog*, their early love of Disney led to them creating magazines specifically for Disney fans. Bringing purpose and passion to print, one might say.

" Stephanie Shuster, CEO and owner, and Danny Shuster, creative director and owner, *WDW Magazine*, *DLR Magazine*, and *DCL Magazine Blog*.

GROWING UP WITH DISNEY

Stephanie Shuster

"I grew up on the West Coast really loving Disney. My parents went to Disneyland on their honeymoon, and I remember them taking my brother and me at an early age. We were a middle-class family, so they had to save for a few years just to afford it.

"We then visited Disney World when I was about 16. When we went on a Disney vacation, my mom and dad just tuned into my brother and me, and each other. So, on those trips we'd have time for more in-depth family time and discussions. For me, I was excited to go to Disney and experience all the rides, candy, and everything, but what really made it special was that time with my family. I saw them in a different light."

Danny Shuster

"We had Disney in my house growing up, but for our vacations we did things like skiing, hiking, and canoeing. I didn't go to a Disney park until I was in my 20s and was dating Stephanie. Then, after we graduated college in 2010, we wandered around Europe and went to Disneyland Paris. It was great for me because I enjoyed theme parks, but most important, I was able to live through her joy of seeing this place she never thought she'd get to see.

"When we got back, we decided to do a 'Disneymoon' when we got married [a 'Disneymoon' is for people who plan their honeymoons at a Disney park]. While on it, Stephanie shared much about the details in the parks with me. In addition, with my dad being an architect, and my appreciation of art design, it gave me my own way into Disney fandom. Plus, when we went to Disney World, we were able to enter what I call 'the bubble,' meaning it was a complete, encapsulated experience. And it was a great test, because though a Disney visit can be physically demanding and plans can change, it can also bring couples and families closer together!"

ON STARTING *WDW MAGAZINE*

Stephanie

"While doing research in 2010 for our first Disney trip, I came across the *Dad's Guide to WDW* website owned by Carl Trent. I realized that it was the type of advice my dad would give me, and I would give others. Then, in 2011 Carl advertised that he was looking for someone to write columns and do social media, so I applied. I was soon hired and ended up writing about half of the content for the site. Next, Carl said he was going to do a magazine, so I started writing for that, too. I also started designing the magazine and began managing assignments, editing, and coordinating photographers, among other responsibilities. As the magazine took off, I also managed its social presence, blog, and finding writers. Then in 2015 Carl brought me on full-time and decided to do a print version in 2018."

Danny

"We knew that to appeal to the Disney audience, we would need to create a quality printed piece. In fact, we've heard many people say that the magazine looks so good that they just can't bring themselves to throw it away!"

Stephanie

"We bought the magazine when Carl retired in 2020. Danny was also able to come on as a full-time creative director—and it has become award-winning."

ON WHY PEOPLE GET SO EMOTIONALLY CONNECTED TO DISNEY

Danny

"I think a lot of it has to do with the environment that Disney designs, one that provides comfort and safety. Stephanie and I have been to the parks and resorts globally and, whether we were in Japan, Paris, Hawaii, or at Disneyland or Disney World, there was always a standard of Disney service that we would be taken care of. And, knowing that all your basic needs will be met, you can more fully live in these experiences. Because you know everything else has been taken care of, it allows you to be playful."

Stephanie

"For me, it's really about nostalgia. It's why, when I see Cinderella Castle, I cry buckets. It's why so many can't wait to see Tinker Bell fly from the tower, having seen her fly at the beginning of *The Wonderful World of Disney* on TV. It's why I will always know that I was able to attain a dream—seeing Disneyland Paris. Like how I remember the very first time I went on the *Matterhorn* at Disneyland as a kid. I had tried ten times before, but I'd always use what I called the 'Chicken Exit.' But I finally did it.

"And it's also how I will always remember when our parents would finally let us stay in the parks for the day as teenagers—on our own!

Even now, thinking back to running around Frontierland—well, it's hard for me to speak because I can feel myself being washed over by those same emotions again."

Then there are the unique stories like this one, where a child inspired by Walt Disney actually ends up working to preserve Walt's legacy. That child was Disney fan and president of Thank You Walt Disney Inc., Dan Viets.

"I remember how *Snow White and the Seven Dwarfs* made a deep impression on me when I was very young," said Dan Viets, attorney and president of Thank You Walt Disney Inc., and co-author of *Walt Disney's Missouri: The Roots of a Creative Genius*. "I loved The Mickey Mouse Club, too.

"Looking back at *Snow White*, it was such a powerful film not just for the Walt Disney Studios, which it built, but for animation in general. Walt had already proven that he knew how to make people laugh with his animation 'shorts,' but he wanted to prove that he could make people cry, too, and feel other emotions.

"In fact, at the premiere of the movie, Clark Gable reportedly cried, along with the rest of the audience, during the scene where the dwarfs are weeping at Snow White's funeral. It takes true art to trigger that kind of reaction.

"I've also been fortunate enough to meet many of the people who were part of the rich history of Disney. For example, I met Annette Funicello when I attended the Disney 75th Legends Awards event at the Walt

Disney Studios in Burbank, California. I also spent an evening at the home of Adriana Caselotti, the voice of Snow White. Adriana was very charming and honored me by playing her grand piano and singing songs from the movie.

"Plus, I had the pleasure of knowing Virginia Davis, who as a child was the star of Walt's *Alice Comedies*, which began in Kansas City. In fact, our organization brought her back to Kansas City several times for Disney-related events. And, I've also had the chance to talk with many other Disney greats like Roy E. Disney, Michael Eisner, and Walt's daughter, Diane.

"Meeting all these people has made my passion for Walt's life and work even stronger, and led me to become part of the nonprofit Thank You Walt Disney Inc. which is committed to saving Walt Disney's Kansas City history and providing a place for art and animation study. This includes our work of preserving and restoring Walt's original Laugh-O-Gram Studio.

"It's more important than ever that we honor the legacy of Walt Disney and his company, including how his pioneering animation spirit moved west through Kansas City all the way out to California. And has since touched the whole world."

OK, now let's grow back down

Grow back down? What exactly does that mean?

Well, for me, it refers to how I felt on that first ride on *Flight of Passage*, and why the title of my blog that described the experience afterwards was "Disney turned this Chicago man into a five-year-old boy." In that moment of wonder, I was a child again. Open to it all. Unjaded. Believing.

The same thing happens to my wife whenever we drive under the "Walt Disney World: The Most Magical Place on Earth" sign. As Gina describes it, she gets a "tickly feeling in my tummy." Once we drive under the sign, she adds, "Though it looks like an ordinary road ahead, it actually takes us to another world. In fact, right away even the large road signs look different, as if they're animated." When I asked if she feels like a little girl at that moment, she simply answered, "Definitely."

And that is what Disney does to us after it has inspired us, taught us, given us a way to explore and grow up. It grows us right back down again. To feel what it's like to see the world again through a child's eyes, to approach a puddle with no intent of going around.

Maslow also shows up in the growing back down. Because as adults become child-like, they give themselves permission to let go of the worries of the day and then play and create. But create in a new way, without worrying about the outcome, like whether the new report they just turned in will get them a promotion. And, in the process of growing back down, we often remember who we are, what we care about, and what we love to do. Oh yes, and by becoming child-like, we also begin to catch glimpses of the top of the pyramid: transcendence. More on that later.

And sometimes that line from childhood to adulthood makes its way right back to childhood as it did for Disney historian Nathan Eick. His story shows how a simple spark, like a visit to Disneyland and seeing Walt's name, ignited a career that continues to touch others and helps him see the world not only through the eyes of his child, but with the eyes of *a* child.

"Growing up in Southern California, I went to Disneyland pretty much every year with my family," said Nathan Eick, Disney historian, former Disney Cast Member, and current senior writer for a financial counseling and education company.

"My mom loves Disney and wanted to instill that enthusiasm in her children. On the first trip there, I fell in love with it almost immediately. Through its sense of space and design, the park transported me to other places and times—and I took everything in. And all around the park, I kept reading the unique words 'Walt Disney,' so I asked my mom, 'What's a Walt Disney?'

"It just so happened that we were on Main Street when I asked my question, and my mom spied *The Walt Disney Story* marquee in front of the *Opera House*. So, we made a beeline for the building and mom saw a painting of Walt in the lobby. She placed me right in front of it. 'He's Walt Disney,' she said.

"That painting helped me understand, on a high level, who Walt Disney was—the guy who started everything. From that day on, I had a steady diet of Disney books and films along with annual trips to 'The Happiest Place on Earth' (eventually 'graduating' to Annual Passholder at the age of 13).

"In 2000, when I turned 18 and started attending college, I got a part-time job at the Merchandise division at Disneyland. Then in 2005, I joined Guest Relations and led some of the park's guided tours. I loved giving the *Walk in Walt's Disneyland Footsteps* tour the most. Because of my extensive knowledge of Disney, I was asked to contribute to a rewrite of the script.

"By 2006, I landed a role with Disney Live Entertainment, where I befriended Stan Freese, who became one of my key Disney mentors (Stan is the author of *Music, Mayhem, and the Mouse: My Tubazar Life*). Stan started with Disney in 1971 as the first leader of the Walt Disney World Marching Band, then transferred to Disneyland three years later and eventually became one of the park's talent booking directors.

"Then in 2016 I moved to Creative Development as Live Entertainment's first dramaturge. In a professional theater company, the dramaturge does the research for each production. I also created a newsletter, helped the show writers, and even got to write for Bill Rogers and Camille Dixon, the 'voices' of Disneyland and Disney California Adventure, respectively.

"At the same time, I became my department's resident historian. This was a particularly exciting piece of my role, as there wasn't as much written about Live Entertainment history when compared to, say, the park attractions or Disney films.

"I left Disney in 2022, but even though I no longer work there, I am still involved with, and consult on, Disney-related projects, write about Disney history on my blog, and am active in the Hyperion Historical Alliance (a non-profit organization for Disney history scholars).

"Disney has meant a lot to me throughout my life and continues to do so. When my wife, Lauren, and I had our daughter Penelope in 2019, I got the chance to share that passion with her—just like my mom did with me. In fact, we took Penelope to Disneyland for the first time when she was just three weeks old!

"I was so excited as Lauren and I sat on the bench with Penelope on the *King Arthur Carrousel*. Even though Penelope slept through the ride and would never remember anything from that day, I would remember it forever. I had always dreamed of sharing the magic of the parks with my kids and it was finally happening.

"A few months later we got Penelope's first picture with Mickey Mouse. As Lauren held her, Mickey came in close, Penelope's eyes widening with delight. She then grabbed Mickey's nose and held it inquisitively. Seeing Penelope react to Mickey was very poetic. Mickey was a character I had loved my whole life...and there I was—sharing that feeling, that sense of magic and wonder with my baby girl. It took me right back to that moment in the Disneyland *Opera House* with my mom."

Yes, there is something about being a parent taking your child to a Disney park, movie, Broadway or Disney On Ice show, on a Disney cruise, or to some other event, that can quickly have you seeing double or more. You see the world simultaneously through your adult eyes, your child's eyes, and through your own eyes as a child. Throw in grandchildren—like when Gina and I were able to watch the end-of-the-evening *Harmonious* show at EPCOT with our family, which included our new granddaughter—and you're likely talking about needing at least trifocal lenses for all those perspectives.

To get a sense for how these different perspectives come together, check out Ashley Martinez's story, followed by her son's. Two perspectives of Disney World, but even with the differences you'd expect, you can see how they reflect each other in that familiar family way.

"

Ashley Martinez, long-time Disney fan.

"I frequently visit Walt Disney World, and every time I go I still get goosebumps! Some of my fondest memories, and trust me, there are many to mention, are with my children.

"When my son, Jacob, was 15 months old, we had some truly magical moments. He knew his favorite characters from movies and books, ran to hug them (often tripping over his own feet to get to them quickly), and called out to them at the parades by name.

"We also waited for him to receive his first-ever haircut at the *Harmony Barber Shop* at the Magic Kingdom. It was something I wanted to experience with him and is highly recommended! He rode the rides he was able to, laughing and screaming with excitement. The first time he watched the fireworks was special, as he clapped and danced along with the music.

"My daughter had to wait a bit longer to experience the magic in person due to the pandemic. When we took her to the Magic Kingdom last summer, it took me back to the memories of her brother's first visits. She looked at Cinderella Castle with sparkles in her eyes. When we met our favorite princesses, she ran over and looked at them with wonder in her eyes.

"When someone asks why we vacation there so often, I tell them you are taken to a different world when you arrive. A world of wonder, a world of magic, a world of pure enjoyment! As someone who feels like a child themselves when they walk through those gates, experiencing Disney with their own children is just magical. I thank Cast Members for giving guests like me the true pleasure of knowing there is still magic and wonder in this world for us to enjoy."

Jacob, age 7, shorter-time Disney fan.

"I love Disney World so much because of the castle and the rides!! I love the castle because it's so pretty and the fireworks are so big. My favorite ride is the *Tomorrowland Speedway* and 'the mining one.'

"My favorite thing about Disney is all the ice cream I get to eat! When we went last year I rode ALL the rides because I was finally big enough. I rode *Big Thunder Mountain* three times in a row and *Mine Train* four times. I can't wait to go back to see 'Star Wars land' and meet baby Grogu."

Then if you really want to make things interesting, consider that in order to grow back down, sometimes people only have to remember themselves as children experiencing Disney to feel like that child again. Even to the point of that memory being from very early in their lives—like Matthew Krul, a fan, influencer, and former Disney Cast Member.

"I think back to the first time my girlfriend (now my wife) and I went to Disney World. Since we had only been dating about six months, and I am obviously very passionate about being there—having grown up with Disney, I considered it a strong start to the relationship," shares Matthew

Krul, founder and host of *Imagination Skyway*, and former Disney Cast Member.

"I was particularly excited to go to EPCOT with her since it had a special place in my heart. The thing I didn't foresee was that experiencing it with her would be like seeing it again for the first time. We went to all my favorite pavilions, like France and Mexico, and attractions like *Test Track, Soarin,' Maelstrom* (since replaced by *Frozen Ever After*), and *Spaceship Earth*. And then we capped the night off with *Illuminations*.

"Now today, we're looking forward to seeing the parks new again with our baby daughter. Of course, some people wonder why anyone would bring a baby to a Disney park. To answer that, I'd share an important realization I had recently.

"As a child, I had a recurring dream of being in a big, blue two-story room with a large glass ceiling. I assumed it was the local mall, but realized over time that it couldn't have been. Then, as an adult, while doing research about The Land pavilion at EPCOT, I realized that the recurring dream was actually a memory I had of sitting in that pavilion as a baby with my parents. Which began to bring everything full circle for me. Because that pavilion has always been special to me—and I finally understood why. Further completing the circle, while later doing my podcast, I shared my realization with two Imagineers who worked on the pavilion.

"Looking back, that realization gave me goosebumps at the time—and it's giving me them again right now as I share this. So there you go, the first moment I recall from my life is a Disney moment. That pretty much says it all."

Finally, here are two stories that, at first glance, feel different. One starts at a young age. One as an adult. But as you read, notice where the pivotal moment happens for each—on Main Street in Disney World and Disneyland, respectively. And notice how, in that moment, they seem to see with a child's eyes. A moment that changes the direction of their lives, including becoming authors who write about Disney. With that, I give you Steve Barrett and Richard Snow.

"My first real experience with Disney, outside of watching their movies, came in 1989 when I was about to attend a medical conference in Orlando. I had been to Disneyland once as a kid but had never been to Disney World," said Steve Barrett, urgent care physician and author of the *Hidden Mickeys* series of books and *The Hassle-Free Walt Disney World Vacation*.

"After learning more about Disney World from a neighbor in Oklahoma, my wife decided to join me, along with our six-year-old son, so they could visit while I was at the conference. I thought it would be like other theme parks, so I wasn't that interested.

"Before leaving for Orlando, though, my wife bought *Birnbaum's Official Walt Disney World Vacation Guide* for herself and *The Unofficial Guide to Walt Disney World* by Bob Sehlinger for me. I skimmed the entire book during the flight, and after landing immediately decided to not attend the conference and instead go with my wife and son to explore Disney World. Something about it intrigued me.

"The next morning, I clearly remember walking into the Magic Kingdom, walking through the tunnel under the train station, and stepping onto

HOW DOES DISNEY DO THAT?

Main Street. As soon as I did, I stopped and said to myself, 'Ok, this is heaven.' Somehow, right then, I knew it would be an escape for me. I couldn't believe a place like that existed. And, really, the rest of that trip was like a dream. Truly a magical experience.

"From that point on, I connected with Disney and read everything about it and Walt Disney that I could. In fact, I loved it so much that, in 1998, I told my wife, 'I've got to move there.' So we moved to Orlando, and I've never looked back. Oh, and yes, I go at least once a week to Disney World.

"Really, I wish I could just live there. I feel a real connection there. I love to watch the guests and the kids and how they react. And to see how that environment Disney created brings the child out in anybody—the wonder, the exploring. It truly is a wonderful world of Disney. At this point, I've visited the U.S. parks and Tokyo Disney and have also cruised on all the Disney ships except the Disney *Wish*.

"Looking back, my wife often talks about how that one moment on Main Street changed the whole trajectory of my life, and she's right! In fact, it led directly to me writing the books I have about Disney. And what's so great is how she supports me in all of it. In fact, she handles all the social media for the *Hidden Mickey Guy* website and books. And, really, our whole family is connected to, and by, Disney World.

"You know, I've really thought about why Disney World has had that effect. For me, it offers a form of escapism. I feel a release there. When I feel stressed at work (as a physician), I just need to think of being on *Peter Pan's Flight*. It then instantly takes the weight off my shoulders.

"My wife sometimes also asks me why I love it so much, too. And I tell her it elevates my spirit and makes me feel like a kid again.

"Of course, Disney World holds a real draw for adults as well as kids. As I said about myself, I believe it has to do with escaping the stresses of life and reconnecting with the inner child in us. And actually, I see that in a lot of adults at the parks, like, for example, a grown man walking around with a crazy hat. Would he ever wear that hat outside of Disney World? Probably not. But he would there because his inner child has been released.

"And really, Disney strikes that same chord with all humanity, which is why it has such a universal appeal. For example, when we went to Tokyo Disneyland, we saw just how much the Japanese love Disney. Every morning, right after the rope would drop, they would run to get in, all giddy with excitement. And that's true for Disney all around the world.

"It also applies when the rest of the world comes here. For example, my son was working with several teammates from Bulgaria who had come to Orlando for a meeting. And what was the one place they most wanted to visit? Yes, Disney World!

"It's that kind of enthusiasm that also led me to write my Disney vacation book and then the *Hidden Mickeys Field Guide* series. One of the real honors I've received connected to the books was when an Imagineer told me they were going to put my caricature in the food court at the All-Star Sports Resort. If you go there, you may just find a 'Hidden Steve.' (It's on the last design pane near the rear exit. The 'Hidden Steve' is sitting in the stands behind hockey player Minnie Mouse. He's also holding a *Hidden Mickeys* book and there's a classic Mickey on his shirt.)

"Looking around now, I think Walt would be happy with what he sees with his company, with the amazing things the Imagineers have done, the rides, all the attention to detail, the people walking around his parks, all of it. And, really, seeing the love he has helped create for our world."

"As a boy, I loved amusement parks," said Richard Snow, author of *Disney's Land*, among many other books, and former editor-in-chief of *American Heritage* magazine. "I grew up in Westchester, a suburb of New York, and Playland was our nearest amusement park. Later, I badgered my father to take me to Coney Island. But then we got our first television set and Walt Disney appeared on it and started telling me about Disneyland and that swept everything else away.

"So in 1959, when I was 12, I whined my parents into sending me out to my aunt and uncle in Los Angeles, and they took me to Disneyland, where Disney had just finished the *Matterhorn, Monorail*, and submarine ride. And it was just as I thought it would be.

"I was instantly enchanted.

"In fact, Disneyland surpassed every expectation I had. I even remember marveling at how they made Mickey Mouse's image out of flowers on the slope of greenery leading up to the train station, and believe me, 12-year-old boys don't typically notice, much less marvel, at flowers!

"One of the moments earlier in the visit that sticks out for me was when my aunt, uncle, and I went on the *Submarine Voyage*. My uncle had been involved with submarines and making torpedoes during World War II, and he thought the ride was very realistic. In fact, when we were climbing out of the hatch, he said 'It even smells right.' Yep, Disney is in the details.

"After we had gone on several rides, my aunt and uncle then turned me loose! And everything was wonderful, including the *Peter Pan* ride, the *Jungle Cruise*—even the teacups.

"But the thing that stayed with me most was right at the end of the day, back on Main Street when it began to get dark, and the lights started coming on along all those gingerbread buildings. There was a horse car clopping quietly by, and I could hear the whistle of the steam train as it pulled into the station. Suddenly it was twilight on a tranquil American small city street in 1908. And I thought, 'I want to stay here forever.'

"Then, in a way, I managed to do just that, in that it got me interested in American history, particularly at the turn-of-the-century, which expanded into a fascination with all American history. And I'm so grateful to Walt for that, and to everyone at Disney who do so many things well, which means so much to me now as well as to that young boy on that day, where I remember it feeling like the people at Disneyland went out of their way to give me a good time—more than they even had to. Which made me feel that they must have liked me. And I certainly liked them!

"In that moment on Main Street, of course, as a boy I couldn't have put all that into words. I was just getting a total feeling of comfort and promise. And that feeling still hasn't left me."

And really that's it, right there. In those two moments that are so much the same.

The *something*.

The something that would cause two different people—one, an adult who decides to go to Disney World instead of attending the professional conference he had made the trip for, and the other a young boy who does everything he can to make it across the country to Disneyland—to both stand on a Disney Main Street and literally have their lives transformed.

The same something, I believe, that turned me into a young boy on *Flight of Passage*. And turns my wife into a little girl every time we drive under the Disney World sign. That has done the same for millions upon millions around the world for 100 years now.

So, what can we call it?

Brand loyalty? Well, yeah, sure, if you're writing a corporate press release.

Customer delight? Yep, that will do the trick for your marketing report.

Or maybe, just maybe, it's something we can't quite define, something that can help a child become an adult who becomes a child again, connecting them back to themselves, others, and ultimately the whole world.

Might I suggest a five-letter word famously connected with Disney?

Starts with "M" and ends with "C."

Yep, that feels right.

Questions

1. What was your earliest Disney memory?
2. Do you ever watch home movies from your Disney trips? If so, did anything surprise you about them?
3. If you're a parent, how did it feel to see your child accomplish something with Disney they might not have known they could do?

4. Have you had the experience of becoming a child again with Disney? What was happening when you did?

5. What does Main Street in a Disney park or boarding a Disney Cruise ship mean to you?

6

Growing Together, Part of a Bigger Story

"It all started from a daddy with two daughters, wondering where he could take them where he could have a little fun with them, too."

Walt Disney

A simple stone became something much more on one of our Disney trips.

In 2002, Jeremy received a "wishing stone" from his fifth-grade teacher as an end-of-school-year gift. As his teacher was handing them out to the class, he explained that if they rubbed the stone and made a wish on it, that wish would come true. (Yes, a little risky on the teacher's part, but a whole lot of fun for the kids. For the parents? Well, we'd just have to figure it out!)

After Jeremy told us about the gift, my wife got an idea. Knowing how much our kids wanted Gina's parents to join us on our trip to Disney World a few weeks later, and that they would in fact be surprising us there, Gina decided to bring the stone along. Why? Because moms are born not only with the innate wisdom to know exactly how many green beans are left on your plate, but also the ability to see deep into the future.

> The whole green bean thing got me thinking about the best animated Disney moms, so I did what any able-bodied writer would do who was intent on researching it to the best of their abilities. Yep, Google again. And here are just a few of the names I found: Bambi's mom from *Bambi* (and, yes, her death can still be felt by generations), Eudora from *Princess and the Frog*, Perdita from *101 Dalmations*, Mrs. Jumbo from *Dumbo*, Queen Elinor from *Brave*, and Helen Parr from *The Incredibles*. Any others you'd add to the list?

During our trip, while eating with the kids at the *1900 Park Fare Restaurant* at the Grand Floridian, Gina brought the stone out and asked the boys if they wanted to wish on it to see if their grandparents would show up (Gina's parents had, in fact, arrived and were waiting just outside the restaurant). At that point, Jeremy gave the stone to Matthew to make the wish, delegating appropriately. After the wish...wait for it... their grandparents walked in! And I'm guessing you can imagine the look on our children's faces (including Alexandra, who was almost two) when they did. As Jeremy recalls, "It was so exciting to see them!" And Matthew adds now, "It was one of the happiest moments of my life!"

After the trip, I shared the "wishing stone" story with *Disney Magazine*, a precursor to writing about my experience on *Flight of Passage* years later. Yes, in both instances, one of my first inclinations was to share the story. Because that's what we humans do.

"My love of Disney came to me later in life, after I had children," said Steve Boettcher, owner of Boettcher Media Group and a producer of the PBS *Pioneers in Television* series, which included interviews with Dick Van Dyke, Tim Allen, and Robin Williams, and production of the *Betty White: A Celebration* documentary.

"Going with them to the parks, seeing that awe on their faces...well, that was something. And when they were little, I remember walking around the parks with our stroller. It was like our own little covered wagon, with all the things inside and everything hanging off it, like water and snacks.

"When I ask our kids now what they most remember about Disney World, they said they remember the anticipation. Like getting on a Disney bus in the morning to go to one of the parks. And all the energy on that bus!

"Of course, there was also the flip side. Coming back to the resort at the end of the day on the bus. After the fireworks. After a long day at the parks under the Florida sun. We were drained and exhausted, but it was a good exhaustion because of all the fun and excitement we'd had. To this day, I still can remember the lullaby-type music playing on the bus with everyone sleeping, myself included! That love of Disney also stayed with our kids as they grew up. My son, for example, worked in the Disney College Program.

"Really, there are ten great places in the world our family loves to visit. Disney is one of them...I don't remember the other nine."

In the years after the "wishing stone" trip, as Disney does, it continued to bring my family together. Like on a Disney World trip in 2013 when we met up with my sister, Bobbie, and her family.

But really, Disney's ability to bring families together through its parks shouldn't come as a surprise when you think back to the origin story of Disneyland. Where, as Walt Disney himself famously—and almost mythically, at this point—explained, while at Griffith Park in Los Angeles one Saturday, one of the "Daddy Days" that he'd spend with his young daughters, Diane and Sharon, he sat on a bench eating peanuts, watching them ride the park's carousel. As he did, he imagined a place where families could have fun together. And, again, according to Walt, right then and there, he began to dream Disneyland into existence.

From "This Old-Timey Merry-Go-Round in Griffith Park Inspired Walt Disney to Create Disneyland" by Lindsay Blake in *Los Angeles Magazine* at lamag.com:

"The Griffith Park Merry-Go-Round (at 4730 Crystal Springs Drive in Los Angeles) was built in 1926 by the Spillman Engineering Company. Commissioned by the Spreckels family, it was originally housed at the Mission Beach Amusement Center in San Diego but was moved to its current location in 1937. The merry-go-round is comprised of 68 hand-made horses, all of which jump, and a custom-built Stinson 165 Military Band Organ that plays more than 1,500 songs. It's the only full-size Spillman carousel still in operation today."

That magical moment

I believe, though, that something else happened *right before* Walt began imagining Disneyland. I believe he felt something. Something he might not have even realized he was feeling.

What was it?

Well, to answer that, please indulge me for a minute.

Let's imagine we're Walt in that moment. Sitting on that bench. Munching on those peanuts. Listening to the carousel's organ. Watching his daughters going round and round as they smiled and laughed.

What do you *think* he was feeling right then?

Relaxed? Yep, especially being away from the hustle and hurry of his studio.

Happy? Another yes. To be spending time with your children as they're having fun. Well, yeah, that's an easy one.

Loving? I don't think it's a big stretch to say that a dad who was always looking for things to do with his daughters—and took the time to do those things even when he led a major company—loved them.

Wanting to be more involved? Yes, his girls were having fun, but isn't it possible Walt wished he was having the fun more directly with them, and not just sitting on a bench watching? Especially because he always showed how he wanted to be "in the action" with them, playing, telling stories, reading...

Then, if his next thought was that he wanted to create a place where families could have fun together, might we guess that those feelings he was feeling (relaxation, happiness, love, and wanting to be more involved) felt like family to him? Something that, as we know historically, he didn't get a lot of as a child and always seemed to be creating for himself and others.

Meaning that Walt's desire for more of that feeling, for himself and others, led directly to what he wanted to do next—build a place where it could happen.

Now, can I prove all this? Of course not. But as a father of three and grandfather of one, who has felt these types of feelings many times watching my own children and granddaughter, and a writer who wants to share his stories, I can *feel* it's true.

Theron's Keys #6: How designers think about family

Whenever we Imagineers would think about guests, we would think about them in the widest demographic possible, whether that was individuals and couples traveling to Disney parks, or large multi-generational groups traveling together, like a family that included parents, their children, the grandparents, possibly aunts and uncles, their children, and more.

Yes, as designers we don't create an experience in a vacuum. Whoever can come, can come. So you always take into consideration who you're designing for, and you want it to resonate with as many people as possible, across multiple generations.

For example, if you were designing an attraction, is there a nostalgic moment for the adults? A moment of discovery for the children? Do adults get to re-experience part of it through their children's eyes? Or are they all experiencing it for the first time together?

Another example. If you're creating a play area, it needs to have soft surfaces for the children, but still must be able to be navigated by older people who might have mobility concerns. As an experience designer, you have to create the attraction to accommodate the whole family as much as possible.

Another thing that Imagineers, really everyone at Disney, were mindful of was deciding on when to replace something older, like an attraction, which was likely important to an older generation, with something new, which could be exciting for a younger generation. In fact, this was one of the topics I was asked about the most when I was an Imagineer, since it's such a challenge—balancing nostalgia with progress.

Really, the challenge exists because Disney is so good at building strong emotional connections with its guests and creating enduring memories based on so many different types of experiences. Because of this, when something goes away, fans and guests tend to take it personally. After all, the Disney park has become an extension of their homes; they likely travel there frequently, and they may feel a real sense of ownership of the park and the experience, something that can be seen when a guest simply sits on a bench in one of the parks and watches the fantasy world unfold in front of them.

That is why, if an attraction is removed, it can be hard for guests. But, in the end, many of them do understand it's a business, and there aren't endless resources to keep an attraction open and maintained, especially if it isn't being visited by as many people. After all, a Disney park isn't intended to be a museum.

Fortunately, Disney is also very good at understanding what their audience wants and doesn't want—using surveys, focus groups, and other methods. Plus, they really understand their characters and stories. Of course, you're never going to please all the people all the time, but you can try.

Another way Disney honors the past but still progresses is by incorporating past attractions into new ones. For example, at Disney Springs, when we opened *Jock Lindsey's Hangar Bar*, we incorporated many elements of the beloved *Adventurers Club* that Joe Rohde led the creative on for Pleasure Island (which became Downtown Disney which became Disney Springs). This included bringing the entire *Adventurers Club* cast back for the grand opening of the *Hangar Bar* so we could honor them. It was like a family reunion.

As you can see, like Walt, our mindset was to carry that feeling of family on in everything we did.

From the Disney Wiki at www.disney.fandom.com:

"The *Adventurers Club* opened with the rest of Pleasure Island on May 1, 1989, as part of a fictional legend about the island's previous owner, Merriweather Adam Pleasure, and back-story describing each of the buildings' former uses. As told in this backstory, the *Adventurers Club* was built by Pleasure as a library and personal museum for his extensive collection of books and artifacts and a place to entertain his fellow explorers and adventurers. Disney's Imagineers, led by head writer, show producer, and show director Roger Cox, and designer Joe Rohde (who later designed Disney's Animal Kingdom theme park), conceived and created the club."

Now, some might wonder. Why did Walt want to share that feeling he was having? Why not just experience it and let that be enough? Well, as I said, that appears to be what we do. When we experience something, the next thing we want to do is share it. So, yes, as we create our story, growing up and back down again, we also look to grow together, to become part of a bigger story. Of family, community, country, and the whole world, both in laughter and tears.

Here are a couple excerpts on why we share from psychologytoday.com.
From "Why Sharing Stories Brings People Together" by Joshua Gowin, PhD:

"When you tell a story to a friend, you can transfer experiences directly to their brain. They feel what you feel. They empathize...As you relate someone's desires through a story, they become the desires of the audience. When trouble develops, they gasp in unison, and when desires are fulfilled, they smile together...When you hear a good story, you develop empathy with the teller because you experience the events for yourself."

From "Listening to Stories: The Power of Story Circles" by Robyn Fivush, PhD:

"When we listen, truly listen, to someone else's story, we understand who they are in a new and different way, we hear their perspective, their interpretation, their understanding of the world and of themselves. Closely listening to others' stories creates a shared moment of compassion. Learning how to tell your story is a critical social tool for individuals; listening to others' stories builds community."

Did Walt succeed?

Well, I'm sure you're thinking that question is rhetorical, right? Of course he succeeded, just look at how big his company is and how long it's been around. But what I really want to get at with my question is something more subtle. Namely, do you think Walt succeeded in sharing that feeling of family with us?

Well, of course, *I* believe that Walt has successfully done that, made it possible for millions upon millions to feel that sense of family and connection. But don't take my word for it. Instead, let's listen to Lou and, once again, from Hank.

"One Disney memory that always chokes me up is when, years ago, my wife and I were watching the *Share a Dream Come True* parade at the Magic Kingdom with our little daughter," said Lou Mongello, author, speaker, consultant, and founder and host of the *WDW Radio* platform.

"To this day, I remember her sitting in her stroller with remnants of her Mickey ice cream all over her face and melting in her hand because she'd forgotten all about it. I was fascinated, and moved to tears, by her being so entranced by her first Disney parade.

"And that's one of the things about Disney that is so powerful. When I can see others, my children, my wife, our family and friends, responding to it in the way I do. It makes me even more excited to share it with them.

"Like when I recently watched my now-18-year-old daughter go on the new Disney *Wish* cruise ship for the first time. Watching her eyes go wide as we walked into the Grand Hall (as I'm sure my eyes were also doing), into something none of us had ever seen before, amazed me.

"Of course, it's also been incredible to feel my own role transform in relation to Disney. First, of course, I was the child and my parents brought me. Then I was the parent bringing my children. And then one day, hopefully, I'll be the grandparent. And that makes me understand what it must have felt like for my parents when they first took me to Disney World in 1971.

"Then, beneath those memories and that transformation is a common thread...the common bond all of us who love Disney have. That there is this place where we can all come together, filled with food and attractions, and everything else, where an adult can become a princess or a pirate or a Stormtrooper.

"Can we explain it? Not really. But it's there. Now, there will be some who just don't get it. Like a few friends I had back in New Jersey who wondered what I was thinking when I sold my house and gave up my career to move down to Florida and focus much of my life on Disney. To them, all I can say is that it's about a feeling.

"You know, the Disney marketing materials never say one of their attractions is the 'tallest' or 'fastest.' No, they focus on the story behind the attraction, and the feelings that detailed story creates. After all, that's the main purpose of Disney, isn't it, to create feelings in us that we then remember."

"I began working in a radio/TV shop during high school and became a weekend DJ at the local radio station," explains long-time Disney fan and retired senior vice president Hank Reed.

"After that, I graduated college, worked my way up to director at a large communications concern, then became a senior VP with a large financial business. I'm also an aspiring writer, working on a book about the many things I have learned in life, places I've visited, and people I have known.

"One of those things is my lifelong relationship with all things Walt Disney. From watching 'Uncle' Walt on Sunday night on a 12-inch black and white screen with my family in the den, to going to Walt Disney World for the first time, and then on to Disneyland. In fact, my wife and I even honeymooned at WDW shortly after we were married and have returned many times to celebrate anniversaries, birthdays, graduations, promotions, and any other excuse that could be found. My daughter and son-in-law also now work at WDW, so the tradition continues.

"One more detail on my daughter. She had wanted to perform with the choir that sings during Christmas at EPCOT. She got to do it! We arranged for her bestie to fly in early before they were both going on a Disney cruise. Her friend surprised her shortly before the performance. That moment brought so many smiles for all of us...the story continues."

Of course, that family feeling doesn't just go one way. Imagine if, for example, you were Diane or Sharon riding that carousel, seeing your dad sitting on that bench, spending the day just with you. How might that feel?

Especially when you consider the amount of dedicated time in general that Walt spent with his daughters, reading, playing with them around the house, acting out stories for them, building them an elaborate backyard playhouse with running water and a working telephone—and even taking the time to notice what their favorite books were.

And of course, on that last point, he did something many other dads may have wanted to do but didn't have the means or knowledge to accomplish—actually acquiring the properties the books were based on, like *The Many Adventures of Winnie the Pooh* and *Mary Poppins* and creating films out of them. How'd you like to give *that* as a birthday gift to your kid?!

To paraphrase the Walt Disney Family Museum's Spotlight Talk: "P.L. Travers' Mary Poppins" at www.waltdisney.org:

"...when the Silly Symphonies were in their prime and Mickey Mouse was around six years old, publisher Eugene Reynal sent

Walt a copy of *Mary Poppins* after the story was first published in 1934. Inside of the cover, Mr. Reynal inscribed, 'To Walt Disney—Not another 'Mickey' but I think you should like our Mary.' Ten years later, Walt learned that his daughter Diane enjoyed reading about Mary's adventures. Soon after, Walt and his brother Roy began to reach out to P.L. Travers about adapting her tale into a feature film, through one-off conversations that occurred throughout two decades. While convincing her to work with them on a screen adaptation was hard work, the Disney team finally succeeded after they first granted Mrs. Travers the right to approve the final script.

"(The Disney movie) *Saving Mr. Banks* begins at this point in the filmmaking process, focusing on the creative differences between Mrs. Travers and the Disney team...Plenty of hard work was required to bridge these creative differences, which probably resulted in significant amounts of stress. As hinted in *Saving Mr. Banks*, the source of this stress might have come from the pride and protection Mrs. Travers felt for the character of Mary Poppins, who was not unlike what Mickey Mouse was to Walt."

And, there again, in Walt's actions with his daughters, is *that* feeling. Between a parent and their child. Or between an adult and any child they love and are loved by. A feeling that I believe long-time Disney fan and *How Does Disney Do That?* Facebook group member Joseph Davis captures perfectly in his story, from a child's point of view this time, especially in the simple but profound way his father, a train operator at Disney World, helped him get over his fear of monorails.

"My Disney story really started with my dad, Bill," said Joseph Davis, long-time Disney fan and project maintenance lead.

"We were living in Michigan, and in 1981, a year after retiring, he and my mom packed up us five kids and we moved to Florida. My mom found a teaching job and my dad taught and also worked at Disney World.

"When he started at Disney, he had two choices: be a skipper on the *Jungle Cruise* or a train operator. He chose the train. And that's how I got into trains, including building scale models of all four trains on the *Walt Disney World Railroad*—the "Walter E. Disney," the "Roy O. Disney," the "Lilly Belle," and the "Roger E. Broggie."

"Once we were living in Florida, we would often go to Disney World. When we did I would ride the trains, and once a day get the chance to sit up front in the cab with my dad. He'd let me ring the bell and blow the whistle at times, too.

"I also remember how we'd go see the monorails. And with the monorails, though it's funny in hindsight, I remember being scared the first time I saw one in person. I knew they ran on electricity, and I was worried I'd get electrocuted. So my dad just had me put a finger on the monorail body itself to see that it was safe to get on.

"That love of trains also led to me and my dad joining The Carolwood Society which preserves the railroad legacy of Walt. Most of all, when I work on my small replicas of the trains, it takes me right back to those times I rode with my dad. I feel connected to him, to Disney World, to Walt, and to all those who helped him bring his railroads to life."

As we know, that feeling of family also crosses and connects generations, from parents to grandparents to great-grandparents, extended families, and everyone in between. Something I learned firsthand after our granddaughter, Penelope, was born. Especially as I looked down at her in her stroller as we first walked out onto Main Street at the Magic Kingdom, immediately reflecting back to looking at Alexandra in her stroller over twenty years before. Right then both moments became one...and something more. But I'm guessing you get that.

And you know someone else who gets it? My barber, Luis. (Well, Luis is my barber in Florida; my barber in Illinois is my brother-in-law, Markus, who just loves the Disney Dining Plan—and yes, it is cool to have two barbers. I feel like a celebrity. And if you can't tell, I talk to *everyone* I know about their Disney stories.)

> "I have a new grandson. I told my daughter there were two 'firsts' that I wanted to have with him. One was giving him his first haircut. The second was going along on his first visit to Disney World."
> —Luis Bernier, barber at Classique Barbers, Disney fan, and the author's barber.

And when we say Disney crosses generations, by definition we're saying that it also transcends time, linking us to those who came before. Keeping someone present to us who no longer is. Yes, I know this starts to sound a bit spiritual, and you know what, that's ok, because really isn't "spiritual" just a wishing stone's throw from "wonder"? To find out, let's give our ear to Scott.

"My Disney story centers around my dad, who grew up in Nebraska," said Scott Minks, host of *Hangin' at the Hangar Bar* Disney-related podcast, and manager of learning effectiveness at a large insurance company.

"When he was about eleven, he developed polio. After that he was in the hospital for about seven months, during which time he lost the use of his right leg.

"Interestingly, as I grew up, I didn't even really notice his crutches. He was such a strong man, which he worked to teach me about. During my childhood he and my mom took us on our first trip to Disneyland. It was literally like the *National Lampoon's Vacation* movie. We were in our old family Chrysler K-car and drove from southwest Kansas all the way to Anaheim. My brother was fifteen at the time and was just learning to drive, so that made the trip *very* interesting.

"When we got to Disneyland, I went on the *Mad Tea Party* ride with my older brother. He was big and strong and got that cup spinning fast. Really fast. So fast that even thinking about it now makes me queasy. Then we had a great day, though I didn't remember many specifics of it for quite a while.

"In 1992, when I was sixteen and on the first day of spring break, my dad, who was fifty at the time, went on a business trip and quietly passed away from heart and lung failure brought on by the polio.

"When I got older I married Candice, a self-proclaimed 'Disney nut.' In 2005 we made our first trip to Disney World together. It was so much more than I expected. Since I didn't have a lot of memories from my earlier trip there, I wasn't expecting it to be familiar. But there was definitely something comforting about being there. It was so much more than I thought it would be, so exciting, with all the sights, the smells, even the music.

"And really, Disney is one of those things where the deeper you go, the more you get connected to it. And that same thing happens with their other offerings, like going on a Disney cruise, where the Cast Members and service bind you to it. Yes, the magic that happens at Disney is different from anywhere else in the world.

"In 2018, Candice and I went to Disney World again. While there we happened to stop at the *Frontierland Shootin' Arcade*. I'm still not exactly sure why I wanted to stop, but I did. So I got a quarter and did some shooting. Then my wife and I went to enjoy the rest of the park. But somewhere, in those next few minutes, it hit me and a memory of sitting on my father's lap at the *Frontierland Shootin' Exposition* in Disneyland on that long-ago trip came flooding back to me.

"As it did, I remembered how my mom, brother, and I pushed my dad around in his wheelchair that day. Along the way, we stopped at the shooting arcade, where he let me sit on his lap so he could show me how to aim the heavy gun. And remembering that moment made me remember again what kind of father he was, and how bonding it was to be with him, especially at a place like Disneyland.

"After I remembered that moment, I immediately shared the whole story with my wife. Which then added another layer to the memory, and added Disney World to it, too. Then, after another trip in 2019 to Disney World, my wife and I decided, along with some friends, to start our podcast.

"The amazing thing is how all of it, marrying a huge Disney fan, starting the podcast with her and our friends, and more, continue to connect me back to my dad. He shaped me into who I am today, and I see a lot of who he was in myself. And how all of that is wrapped up in Disney memories."

As you can guess, when I interviewed people for this book and came across stories like Scott's, and so many others, where people talked about how important Disney was to them, especially after losing a parent or sibling, I would often just sit in silence as they talked. Because, really, what else can you say?

It was also a reminder to me that, even when I was just starting out on this journey to figure out how Disney does that, I sensed there was really a bigger meaning behind it. A meaning that came out stronger and clearer with every story I'd hear. And why I continue to say that if Disney didn't exist, we'd need to create it.

Because Disney doesn't just entertain. It heals.

As, in my eyes, it appears to be doing for Zach.

"My mom first brought me to Disney World when I was four. My dad didn't go because he wasn't really into Disney. But that all changed a year later when my mom convinced him to come. And within a half day of being there, he was hooked," said Zach Keller, long-time Disney fan and general manager for an athletics properties company.

"While there, each of us had things we wanted to do, those little moments that made it special for us individually, as well as those we enjoyed as a family. My dad and I liked looking at the windows along Main Street, and my mom liked shopping in those stores! My dad also enjoyed sitting on the benches, soaking it all in. From that point on, we went to Disney World for the holidays every year. And there are two things that really stand out for me about those visits.

"One was, as a ten-year-old, loving the *One Man's Dream* museum-like attraction about Walt's life at the Disney-MGM Studios Park (now Disney's Hollywood Studios). The whole thing really pointed out how much Walt had brought to my family—along with his impact on other families. And, yes, I was thinking all that at ten!

"The other thing was in 2001, during a National Tai Kwan Do tournament at Disney World, when we took time to go to the Magic Kingdom. I still remember walking through the gates and being overjoyed, the looks on my parents' faces as they looked at me and the park, and what it felt like to be holding their hands. It was an awesome moment of pure joy.

"Sadly, my dad passed away in 2010, when I was a teenager, and the rest of my family only went a few times after that. Then, about ten years later, both my mother and brother passed away, a year apart. Right before my mom died we took one last trip to Disney World and stayed at the Animal Kingdom Lodge. It meant so much to be there with her.

"Thankfully, some very positive moments with Disney followed. In 2020, my girlfriend and I attended a wedding in Florida and then went the next day to the Magic Kingdom. She hadn't really grown up with Disney as a child like I had. But, like my dad, after being at the park for a day, she fell in love with it, too. Afterwards, she said it was like she was a kid again. A year later I proposed to her in front of Cinderella Castle. For our honeymoon, we're looking to go to Disney's Aulani resort.

"When I'm asked how I'm doing with everything that's happened in my life, I think of how sometimes you're at the cheery end of the Disney movie and sometimes you're in the scene in *Lion King*, where Simba's father dies and he's suddenly alone. For me, Disney helps me remember and appreciate those positive moments even more.

"And of course, I still have the pictures around my house of all of us in matching shirts at Disney World. My mom would take the same shot every time we went in front of the same backdrop. I also have the little Disney crystals my dad bought her. And the only ornaments we have on our tree are from Disney.

"I remember reading the tagline on the *How Does Disney Do That?* online group page that 'If Disney didn't exist, we'd need to create it.' Well, I really believe that."

Pause. Breathe.

It's hard to find just the right words to transition out of Zach's story, so I needed to pause and take a compassionate breath (I imagine you might need to do the same)...Now that we have, I'll ask you to focus on what Zach says near the end of his story—how Disney has helped him heal and stay connected to his family, even those no longer here.

Yes, I'm not quite sure that I knew what I was getting into when I asked myself how Disney does that. But I *am* quite sure that I'm glad I did.

Community isn't common

As with everything we've seen here so far, these perspectives on family and community are shared by both sides of the aisle or "attraction" by the fans and by those who create the Disney experiences, as Theron explained earlier in the chapter.

Yes, it's easy to see how Walt's wanting to share a feeling of family with fans has succeeded. All you have to do is stand in one of the attraction queues, walk through one of the cruise ship restaurants, or jump on a fan Facebook group. The resounding "Yes!" will surround you.

But, to add to Theron's voice, it's important to also hear how that feeling can be found in those entrusted with carrying on Walt's legacy—with helping to bring together people in a way that allows them to put down their worries and pick up their spirits. In someone like Josh Steadman, former Imagineer.

"I grew up on an Idaho farm. And I grew up with Disney. Plus, my mom was very passionate about Disney. I'm sure that helped lead to me wanting to work for the company, especially as an Imagineer," said Josh Steadman, former Imagineer and owner of Steadman Styles, a themed entertainment design company.

"So in 1998, I began that journey by joining the Disney College Program. My first role was at Disney-MGM Studios (now Disney's Hollywood Studios) as a bellhop in the *Tower of Terror*. Next, I was in the *Mulan* parade, worked crowd control at *Fantasmic*, and then joined the Travel Department.

"After that, I joined Walt Disney Imagineering and was mentored at one point by Doris Hardoon, who took on a leadership role on the Shanghai Disney Resort. It really was exciting to work with her on the world's tallest, widest Disney castle there, along with other projects.

"Looking back, I realize that I originally went into theme park design because it gave me an alternate reality. The real world is rough, filled with a lot of darkness, so we often need that. And I believe that an alternate reality, something spectacular, is worth waiting for.

"A great example of an alternate reality is the experience of going to a Disney park. That experience is a combination of eliminating distractions and the negative aspects of life for a while, immersing people in stories, and doing it all in a communal way. You're doing that experience with thousands of other people. Sometimes, in fact, that feeling is *so* strong that it borders on the spiritual. I believe that a designed, curated experience like that, whether it's at a Disney park, in a theater, or anywhere, can change a person and help make the world a better place.

"In many ways, I believe that's what many of us lack today—that communal experience, where we're part of a bigger story together—and that's why we crave it. Inside, we all want to believe that an alternate reality like that can be real. That you can harness that magic, that human need to care, love, and feel.

"And that's what Disney does really well, that separates them. By designing those experiences to tap into that need and what guests want to feel. In fact, that's why Disney fans will experience the things they do. Because there are people working for Disney, like the Imagineers, who care passionately about what they do and what the guests will feel. They're carrying on Walt's legacy. Thousands of other Cast Members, too, are involved, who care about the product being delivered.

"So, that's why I do what I do, too, and why I did what I did for Disney. My purpose, as I see it, is to make people happy and continue to design things that do."

A family by experience

"Family" can mean many things to many people. It can be the family we're born into, or one formed in the variety of ways families form. But it can also describe that feeling that comes from belonging to a community, being on or rooting for a team (just notice the looks in the stands as fans go from elation to grief with their team's fortunes; I should know, I'm a Chicago Cubs fan), from believing in the same thing, or by sharing a similar experience.

Especially when that experience is one of the hardest things a family can face. As Steve Amos shares with us about Give Kids The World Village® and its partnership with Disney, and how both help create that feeling for families so in need of it.

"Like many, my connection to Give Kids The World Village began with the Disney College Program," said Steven Amos, former Disney leader and vice president of advancement at Give Kids The World Village®.

"I started with Disney's program in 2008 and worked at Walt Disney World until 2017 in Operations, Marketing, Guest Experience, and more. My last role was as a producer with Disney's Yellow Shoes in-house advertising agency.

"During that time, I remember working mainly nights at Disney Springs. I didn't have kids at the time, so I started volunteering during the day at Give Kids The World Village in nearby Kissimmee—and it completely changed my perspective.

"In 2017 I began working at the Village, and the opportunity to work for both organizations has been tremendous. When I was at Disney, I saw first-hand how they supported the Village. And then, being with the Village, I saw how strong that partnership is from the other side, too. For example, many Disney Cast Members and former Disney employees volunteer there.

"At the Village, between the *Enchanted Carousel* and other wheelchair-accessible rides, whimsical attractions like *Henri's Starlite Scoops* and *Julie's Safari Theater*, horseback riding, fishing, and dining, anyone visiting the Village might feel as if they'd actually come to a Disney resort! There are also characters, nightly entertainment, private Wish family villas, a wheelchair-accessible pool and splash pad, snoring trees, and the crown jewel of the Village, the Castle of Miracles.

"Inside the castle and adjoining Star Tower, the stars of every Wish child who has visited adorn the ceiling as a permanent reminder of each child's special wish. And all of it is made possible by a caring staff and passionate volunteers who fill up to 1,800 volunteer shifts every week.

"It's difficult to put into words how much magic happens at the Village and during Wish families' visits to Disney World and other attractions. Wish trips help kids build resilience and optimism, and that often starts even before the trip! Wish trips also create cherished memories for Wish families."

We are (all) family

Remember my "wishing stone" story? When I shared it with you at the beginning of the chapter, I'm guessing you got it right away. That you knew just how much it meant to our kids to see their grandparents walk into that restaurant, and because it meant a lot to them, it meant a lot to us, and to their grandparents. And because that happened to all of us at the same time in the place we loved, I'm guessing you know what that felt like, too.

And when I shared the story about Walt watching his girls and asked you to put yourself in his shoes, I'm guessing once again that it wasn't hard for you. That you likely knew how he felt as he watched his children go round.

And as you were reading the other stories in this chapter, about love, loss, excitement, and all points in between, I'm (yes, you guessed it) guessing that you got it then, too.

Why do I feel so comfortable making these guesses? Because...wait for it...you're human. And...wait for it again... so am I. And most of us share the same basic needs (think Maslow), hopes, fears, and desires.

Well, I believe Walt, a great observer of the human condition, knew that, too. And I believe that he knew that if he could tap into those common needs, he could make people feel something and use those same feelings to connect, or reconnect, them to themselves and something bigger.

Us.

Want a quick way to see that basic humanity in action? Go back and read the stories shared in this chapter. Remember, most of the people who gave those stories to me don't know each other. Yet look at how similar the key elements in their stories are. The growing connection to Disney. The shared moments of joy. The quiet moments of grief. And the power of healing.

How does that *happen*? And, by extension, what happens when you then take millions of adults with the same basic human needs and put them in the same resort or on the same cruise for a period of time, one in which they can forget their worries and remember how to be kids again? Along with a whole lot of their kids and grandkids and great-grandkids who don't have to remember—because they're already there?

Want to know how small a world can feel? Just join them.

So with that, let's ask Nathan Eick, Disney historian, who we heard from earlier in the book, to play us out of this chapter right into the next. Where we talk about how a lost purse helps us finally reach the top of the pyramid where a little white sign awaits.

"These Disney moments happen to millions of people every year—a cultural connection from one generation to the next," said Nathan Eick, Disney historian, former Disney Cast Member, and senior writer for an organization that offers financial, career, and personal development solutions.

"Because the Disney parks have been around for almost 70 years, there is a multi-generational affection for these places around the world. For Americans in particular, the parks are ingrained in the cultural zeitgeist. Who today doesn't get a little twinge of nostalgia seeing a star football player cry out, 'I'm going to Disneyland (or Disney World)!' after winning the Super Bowl?

"People remember their childhood visits to the Disney parks with a special kind of fondness, and then they get to relive that feeling all over again in a slightly different way through their children. It's a rite of passage, a way for the generations to bond even though they are separated by technological and cultural thresholds and preferences.

"Young and old, people love Disneyland (even the teenagers who think they're too cool for it). The Disney parks, at their best, have become places that bring everyone together—as Walt intended. People might not see eye-to-eye in the real world—politically, culturally, generationally, and in other ways—but when they enter the worlds of 'yesterday, tomorrow, and fantasy,' all that melts away for a few hours and people reconnect with something we all share as human beings."

Questions

1. What Disney wish would you make upon a "wishing stone"?

2. If you happened to sit down next to Walt while he was watching his daughters on the carousel, what would you ask him?

3. Are there any Disney attractions that are now gone that you miss? Why do you think you miss them?

4. Has Disney ever helped you get through a hard time?

5. Do you agree that Disney fans are like a family?

7

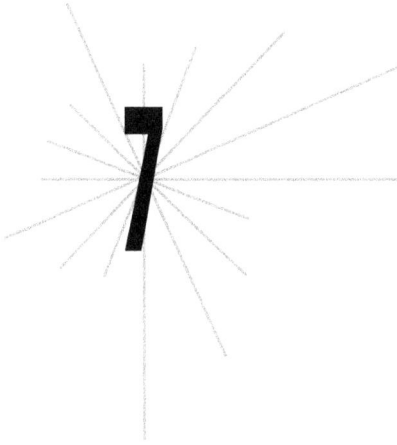

The Wonder Full World of Disney

"Awe is the emotion of self-transcendence."

Jonathan Haidt

O n our 2010 Disney World trip our daughter's purse, like the wishing stone before it, became something more.

Or I should say its absence did.

Gina, the kids, and I had just taken the monorail to EPCOT and were walking through the breezeway under *Spaceship Earth* when Alexandra realized she had left her purse onboard. Now, I immediately knew this was not a good thing. But sensing that a purse is more than a purse, especially to a 10-year-old girl, I didn't quite realize then how much not a good thing it was. So, today I did some research on what a purse means to a young girl. No, not with Google this time. I needed something more powerful. Or should I say someone?

My wife.

"For a young girl, a purse is pretty important," Gina explained to me. "No, actually, it's *very* important! You're at that age where you're trying to be a young woman, and that purse has a lot to do with that."

As she then shared her own personal memories of purses long gone by, I made a mental note: "Yep, purses matter."

So, back to our story.

When Alexandra told us she'd left her purse on the monorail, my first instinct was to think, "Well, there's no way we'll get that back." But obviously, my instinct didn't remember that we were at Disney.

Once I did remember, though, I also recalled that things happen with Disney that don't happen in the "real" world, as if the laws of time and space are somehow suspended. So I told my daughter I'd see what I could do, which really meant what the Cast Members could do. At which point I walked back to the Security Desk at the front of the park and told one of the officers what had happened.

Now, if I did that in the "real world," what do you think the typical reaction would be? Possibly an "Ok, thanks for letting us know. We'll let you know if it turns up." Or "We're sorry. Here's a coupon for 15% off your next purchase."

Which is really just a "no" dressed up in a rented tuxedo.

But, again, I was at Disney, where the typical reaction from a Cast Member is "Yes." Meaning, yes, let me help you, and yes, let's figure out a way, and yes, you're *that* important to us.

So with a smile (and that smile is very important to a guest with a young daughter who just left her purse behind), the security officer made a call to the Transportation and Ticket Center (TTC), the hub in front of the Magic Kingdom where the monorails, buses, ferry boats, and other modes of resort transportation intersect.

After that, as relayed to me by the security officer, the TTC called the captain of the monorail we had been on who, at his next stop, searched every car looking for the purse. Finding it, he then dropped it off at the TTC, where another monorail captain picked it up and then dropped it off at the EPCOT station. And at that point, another Cast Member walked the purse down several levels to the Security Desk where I was standing, just as the security officer finished up his play-by-play.

Can you guess what I was feeling at that moment?

Yep, that. And more.

After all, a place that we loved had just gone that extra mile, and extra monorail, to bring something back that our daughter loved. And yes, as you've likely guessed, we love our daughter bigger than...well...everything. That's a whole lotta love.

Now, for all that to happen, every person along that chain had to not only have been well-recruited and trained and in a company culture that encouraged those actions, but also have that extra special "want to," knowing they all played a big part in a bigger picture. But, if even one of them had decided they didn't want to put in that extra effort for whatever reason—they were tired, didn't feel like it, it wasn't in their job description, etc., etc.—that chain would have been broken and the purse wouldn't have made it back.

But it did. And because of that, the moment was about to get even better.

After thanking the Security team, I walked back to Gina and the kids, still standing near the breezeway...and handed the purse to Alexandra.

She looked at the purse, then up at me.

And I wish I had the words to describe her face right then. But I'm also glad I don't. Because, for some things, words aren't enough.

That was one of those moments.

And if you don't think Disney magic is a thing, think again. Because just as she was looking up at me, the fireworks from EPCOT's *Illuminations* show started going off behind her.

Cue the goosebumps.

To complete the circle, while writing this chapter I asked Alexandra if she remembered how she felt at that moment.

Her response?

"I'm sure I thought it was like magic!"

Yep, cue the new-and-improved goosebumps.

And what word pairs nicely with "magic"?

Wonder.

Paraphrased from dictionary.cambridge.org:

"Magic" (noun)

- the use of special powers to make things happen that would usually be impossible, such as in stories for children
- the skill of performing tricks to entertain people
- a special and exciting quality that makes something seem different from ordinary things

"Wonder" (noun)

- a feeling of great surprise and admiration caused by seeing or experiencing something that is strange and new
- an object that causes a feeling of great surprise and admiration

Which is why I can so easily connect that Disney moment, and so many others our family has experienced, to my moment on *Flight of Passage* where everything else but that experience disappeared and something else, larger, wider, and brighter, opened up. Where, whether it be through the impact of one of its attractions or commonly uncommon customer service, Disney walked me the rest of the way up to the top of Maslow's pyramid, where I found a little white sign with one word written on it in black...

..."transcendence."

"Yes, but what *is* Maslow's 'transcendence?'" I asked myself because, well, I was the only one around as I wrote this.

Not worried about appearances, though, and drawing on my masterful research sessions, I answered back, "Well, James, that's a typically brilliant question. In basic terms, with Maslow's pyramid, 'transcendence' is when, as someone becomes more authentic, they begin to experience uplifting, peaceful moments where they feel part of something bigger, and therefore focus more on how connected they are to everyone and everything. They may also even sense something beyond their senses. Now, of course, that 'bigger' has taken many forms when it comes to human beings. And I happen to believe that one of them is Disney."

(Ok, though that was a great answer, this whole "asking myself a question and then answering it" thing almost gave me a grammatical injury. I won't be doing that again.)

Disney is a bigger thing

Yes, it probably doesn't come as much of a surprise at this point in the book that I believe Disney is one of those bigger things that connects us to others, back to ourselves, and even in some cases—with apologies to Buzz—to infinity and well beyond.

Why do I believe that?

Well, for that answer, similar to what I asked you to do at the end of the last chapter, go back and re-read some of the stories in this book. As you do, notice how often people talk about Disney making them feel connected to their children, grandchildren, parents, spouses and other oh-so-significant others, friends, and even loved ones who are gone.

Also notice how Disney gives us a way to feel the things we most often need to feel and heal the things we most often need to heal, helps children play and find their path, turns adults back into the children they once were, and creates moments of perfectly perfect transcendence, where every so often our fingertips might punch through the sky and reach the stars. And how, all along the way, Disney encourages us to focus on each other, knowing that for Arendelle to survive, we can't live behind a locked bedroom door.

Of course, that something bigger can sometimes start out as something very small. As in a small moment, where one man, watching two daughters, feels something I believe was love and wanted to share that love with others.

A small moment that transcended.

One of wonder.

And of course, that kind of transcendence wears many hats (preferably Goofy ones) and shows up in many ways. As it did for author Lou Prosperi who saw it in the elegance of Imagineering. Elegance that actually made his jaw drop.

"The first time I went to a Disney park was on my honeymoon in 1993," said Lou Prosperi, author of *The Imagineering Pyramid: Using Disney Theme Park Design Principles to Develop and Promote Your Creative Ideas*, as well as related books, plus owner of The Imagineering Toolbox resources inspired by Walt Disney Imagineering.

"On that first day, the moment I most remember was on *Journey Into Imagination with Figment*, where the word 'avalanche' actually became an avalanche and sent rocks cascading around the passageway. At the time, I was working as a game designer and had always been interested in creativity and imagination—but this literally made my jaw drop. Afterwards, I began using Imagineering principles in my role as an instructional designer and published several books on the subject.

"I think one of the main reasons I and so many others are obsessed with Disney and Disney parks is because people associate Disney with happiness and joy. Plus, for many of us, it's more than just fun. For instance, the Imagineers create such an emotional experience for us, one that touches us in a deeper place. In fact, I feel like I'm the best version of myself when I'm there."

"I feel like I'm the best version of myself when I'm there."

Transcendence? Check.

How this book changed course

"What's the tone of the book going to be, James?"

I remember my publisher, Barry, asking me this question when we were talking about the book early in the development process. My response?

"Whimsical."

Or, as Merriam-Webster defines it, "lightly fanciful."

And here's the thing. At the time, I was right.

Because that's how I thought it would feel. Why? Because I knew I'd be writing about Disney's attractions, the fun we've had there as a family, and wishing stones and deciduous forests. Which all led me to believe that the book would turn out to be fun and whimsical.

And I hope it has been a good amount of both of those things for you.

After all, as Mr. Willy Wonka so famously said in *Willy Wonka and the Chocolate Factory*, "A little nonsense now and then is relished by the wisest men." And women. And children. And basically, anyone with a heart.

Willy Wonka and the Chocolate Factory starring Gene Wilder was another movie that felt Disney-like to me as a kid. And of course, as I've learned, because I felt that way, it was very possible that there were Disney connections to it. A child's heart knows.

First, the idea for adapting the book into a film came when director Mel Stuart's ten-year-old daughter read *Charlie and the Chocolate Factory* by Roald Dahl and asked her father to make a film out of it. Sound familiar? Second, Dahl was reportedly not happy with how his book and main character were translated for the film. Again, sound familiar? And Harper Goff, the film's art director, also had a legendary career at Disney in art direction, special effects, renderings for Disneyland and Disney World, and more. Plus, he was a member of the "Firehouse Five Plus Two" Dixieland jazz band made up of Disney animators led by Ward Kimball. Oh, and just for good measure, Goff advised the U.S. Army on camouflage paint during World War II.

But as the book took shape, it also did what creations do. Evolved. Changed direction and form according to what I thought and felt and experienced and remembered as I wrote it, and what I thought and felt and experienced and remembered as I heard others' stories. Plus, it had taken on the character of its quest, the long, sometimes arduous climb up the pyramid.

Which took me right back to what I intuitively knew after first asking myself, "How does Disney do that?" That I wasn't asking a technical question so much as emotional and philosophical ones.

Questions like, how does Disney take its passion and make it mine, while turning a grown man back into a little boy?

How and why did I fall in love with Disney? Where and when did it happen?

How does Disney help someone see that they're the hero of their own story and can be a hero in others' stories, too?

And why is all this so important to us as humans, especially now, in a world that too often feels disjointed and disconnected?

So, yes, the book has been heavier than "whimsical" at times but, candidly, it went where it had to go. And where I did, too. Because, ultimately, I followed my question.

But here's the thing. I do believe that even transcendence can be whimsical, lightly fanciful. Case in point: how I felt on *Flight of Passage* that day. Yes, it made me cry (just a few tears though, please remember!), but they were tears of wonder. And as I've learned, tears of wonder don't hold us down. They help us fly.

Banshees also come in handy.

The many (Goofy) hats of transcendence

With our ongoing conversation between fans and those who create experiences for them, let's now listen in as several former Imagineers share their perspectives on creating moments of transcendence for fans—where a moment can become a memory, and an attraction, a revelation. Where, in fact, designers can bring people to wonder, goosebumps, laughter, and even the tears that take us right back to *Snow White and the Seven Dwarfs*.

In fact, as we hear their stories, it will serve us well to keep that groundbreaking film in mind and ask ourselves why we believe Walt wanted to prove that animation could make people feel something and not just laugh (though making people laugh is an honorable goal indeed).

I believe it's because, like on that park bench, he wanted to share a feeling, to connect. Just as designers do with the experiences they create, as Joe Rohde and his creative team did with *Flight of Passage*, as former Imagineers Ryan Harmon and Paula Dinkel did below, and as Theron unlocks with his next key.

"Growing up, we went to Disneyland on my birthday every year, and I fell in love with it. In fact, I remember being so fascinated that I began collecting books about Walt Disney and wrote book reports about him and the company. He became my idol," said Ryan Harmon, former show writer, Walt Disney Imagineering, and current president and chief creative officer, Zeitgeist Design + Production.

"When I turned twenty, I was studying film and screenwriting while interning at a Studio City production company, but knew that I wanted to create experiences. Fortunately, I met someone who grew up with a producer who worked at the Walt Disney Imagineering (WDI) building in Glendale, California. She called him and he invited me for lunch and a tour.

"When I first set foot in WDI headquarters, it felt like the heavens opened and a ray of white light came shining down on me. I knew that I had found my destiny, my place, my people. After being offered the role of a show design apprentice that summer, I became the assistant for the Disney-MGM Studios team. I was invited to participate in all aspects of the park's design and production over my first two years!

"On that project, I reported to George Head, Bob Weis, Tom Fitzgerald, Richard Vaughn, and others. During my time at WDI, I also got to work with Joe Lanzisero (now executive vice president and creative director at Zeitgeist), Tony Baxter, Rick Rothschild, Chris Runco, Bruce Gordon, David Mumford, and so many other brilliant creative people. It was also an 'open campus' then, so I spent a lot of time sitting with the original Imagineers who worked with Walt, like Claude Coats, Sam McKim, and Herb Ryman. It was mind-blowing for this young, long-haired college kid to be one step away from Walt Disney.

"The most important thing that Joe and I discuss now regarding park and attraction design is the emotion behind what's happening and how we want people to feel who experience them. I know, for instance, that some of the projects I've written or creative directed, including *Mana-tees: The Last Generation* at Sea World Orlando and the *Titanic Official Movie Experience*, made people cry. That tells me something important. I immersed them in a story; I put them through a human experience, and I made them feel something, which inevitably created a lasting memory."

"I was pixie dusted from a very early age. Though at the time, it never occurred to me that someone could make a career at Disney," said Paula Dinkel, former principal show lighting designer for Walt Disney Imagineering and current lighting design consultant, featured in *Women of Walt Disney Imagineering: 12 Women Reflect on Their Trailblazing Theme Park Careers.*

"I then learned about theater in junior high and, since the actors also worked as backstage crew, I learned about lighting and design, including color intensity, motion, and the mixture of color.

"Later, while teaching lighting at USC, I applied to Disney as a lighting designer and interviewed with Rolly Crump, an important name in Imagineering. At the time, he was putting a team together to keep Disneyland bright, beautiful, and magical, while many others at the company were getting EPCOT ready to open. A week after that interview, I was an Imagineer.

"My first day at Disney was amazing. It started with my orientation class and was reinforced when I walked through WED Enterprises (previous name for 'Walt Disney Imagineering') headquarters. There was literally magic around every corner.

"It was a wonderful time. I met all these new people who were also great artists. And I learned more about lighting and the role it plays in storytelling—not just in the theater, but in places like theme parks. Like when you see lights flickering in the windows on *Pirates of the Caribbean*—something you see often in a Disney park. They're flickering because in the time period the story is set, they didn't have steady electric lights. Of course, that sparkle also shows up throughout the parks, as in the case of Disneyland, in the twinkling lights in the trees along Main Street U.S.A. and with the fireworks. Those twinkling lights somehow touch people.

"Overall, with the different experiences we created, we put a lot into how we wanted the guests to feel, how to bring them into the story and follow it along. The script would dictate what kind of emotions we wanted them to feel, like wonder, charm, excitement, trepidation, and surprise. We'd also all discuss the role that lighting would play in the story and help make those emotions happen.

"The importance of lighting can also be seen in the parks as day turns into night, especially during what we called 'Magic Hour.' In fact, the parks actually seem to take on a different personality then. It's the hour of the day when there is enough daylight to still see the buildings, but you can also see the lights coming on. It is also one of the best times to take photographs. In fact, I worked at Disneyland for ten years, and on days when I needed a little extra pixie dust in my life, I'd go to Main Street and watch people as the lights came on. They'd go 'Wow—the lights!'

"Like candles on a cake, lighting gives that extra sparkle. After all, as show lighters always say, 'If we don't light it, they can't see or feel it.'"

Theron's Keys #7: Transcendence is at the end of the rainbow

Transcendence is the "pot of gold" for an experience designer. We want to suspend your disbelief to the point that you no longer believe you're in a theme park going through a created experience. That's why we tell emotional stories—because feeling something can help us suspend that disbelief. And one of the most difficult emotions to elicit through a created experience is wonder—genuine awe, which really is the emotion of transcendence.

Of course, Mother Nature does transcendence well. Just go to a National Park and stand on one of the vistas, and you'll likely get a sense of wonder, looking out at the size of the mountains and the life all around you.

But here's the thing—we tend to be a jaded species. We're extremely knowledgeable. And that prevents us from dropping our defenses, seeing something new and seeing it as wonder. To be child-like in that acceptance of the emotion of the environment and story. To the point that you no longer doubt, but just embrace and believe.

Yes, we experience designers aim for wonder. After all, when you feel it, you have likely also escaped from the pressures of your whole life for a bit, laughed, and had fun—all while locked in a moment that transforms you and becomes an enduring memory. Then what happens next? People say, "That was awesome! I have to experience all of it again!"

And remember, Imagineers usually start out as fans themselves. We love this stuff! And that's why we do what we do in creating experiences: we're chasing that "wonder" experience for ourselves as well...and we do that by constantly looking for new ways to bring that amazement and emotional connection to our stories globally.

As an experience designer, when I'm working on a project and those elements combine in just the right way, and I get that sense of "Wow that's amazing!" I also intuitively know that guests will love it, too. And after thirty years of doing this, I've found that my gut is usually right. However, it takes a whole cross-functional team to really make it right.

At the same time, in leading large teams working on billion dollar, uber-complex projects over a series of years, we've also faced some really hard challenges. But once you overcome those challenges and deliver a new experience, get the guest write-ups, and see how they perceive it, it can be so rewarding! Especially when you and your team worked to ensure guests were able to get those specific experiences.

Looking behind the scenes with Disney, creating an emotional connection with the guest is an unspoken design requirement, just like requirements around maintenance, aesthetics, quality, and profitability. So when I was in Imagineering, we built that into everything we did—to the point that we expected that connection to happen, that guests would be excited, feel wonder, and so on. Of course, sometimes the guest reaction went well beyond what we anticipated. And, for an Imagineering team, *those* are the golden moments, especially when we knew we had poured all our talent and passion into creating that experience.

But does it work?

Imagineers can intentionally design the expectation of transcendence and wonder into their work. So then we ask, "Yes, but does it work, does it create the wonder they seek?" And might it lead to a conversation like this:

Designer: "How did it make you feel?"

Fan: "It made me a little anxious in that spot where the dragon showed up, especially coming right out of the shadows like that, then really happy when the heroes made it back home to save the kingdom. And for a moment or two along the way, I even forgot I was actually on a ride! I can't wait to do it again."

Designer: "Wonderful, because when we designed it, we were hoping you'd feel those things. After all, it's what we felt when we were designing it."

Fan: "Wow, cool. Thanks!"

Designer: "Thank *you*. Without you, it's only an attraction. After all, for it to be an experience, it has to be experienced."

Yes, for any kind of attraction, event, or show to be an "experience," it obviously needs to be experienced by someone. That means the fans and guests are an essential part of the equation. And what does it mean to experience an experience? Well, as I see it (there I go, answering my own question again), in its simplest form, it means to take it in through our senses, and then think and feel about what we've taken in.

And, though thinking has gotten a lot of press in the past (see René Descartes' "I think, therefore I am" and Auguste Rodin's statue, "The Thinker"), really, doesn't it seem like we feel wonder through our senses, even before our thinking can kick in? I know that for me, as I remember my first time on *Flight of Passage*, the sights and sounds and thousands of other incomparable details stick out, but most of all, what I remember best...

...is the feeling.

Fans are the measure

So, ultimately we fans decide if we have felt wonder on a Disney attraction or in another part of the Disney experience. Not everyone will, though the odds are pretty good, especially over time. And of course, if people felt wonder the first time, they might not the next, depending on many factors—like are they preoccupied with thoughts of work or other concerns, are they not riding attractions with their children like they used to, are they worried that the park is closing and they might not make it to the gift shop for those hard-to-find Halloween Mickey Ears, and so on and so on.

Yes, wonder is a delicate thing. Imagineers and Cast Members can put all the pieces in place, but ultimately it's up to us. No pressure, though. If you don't feel wonder on this Disney attraction or in that Disney show, I can pretty much guarantee that wonder is waiting for you just around the far corner of the castle.

Or right in front of it. Especially if you take a breath and the time to notice.

Why the castle?

Because, if there's one place at Disney parks all around the world you're pretty much guaranteed of seeing looks of wonder, it's when guests see that park's castle for the first time. As they do, their eyes change. Children see fantasy become reality, as the castle they've seen at the beginning of Disney movies comes to life (of course, not every Disney castle is Cinderella Castle, but every Disney castle is amazing), and adults instantly become children again. Oh, yes, and as I've heard and seen with so many, they often cry.

Why do people cry when seeing the castle for the first time—either on that particular trip or any other?

Well, I believe it's because, whether it's a Disney castle or a lost purse returned, it confirms that fairy tales can come true. Something promised that we desperately want to believe in. Hope. Goodness. Optimism. Belonging. Kindness. Belief that there is a great big, beautiful tomorrow, while today is quite something, too, and yesterday is well worth remembering.

As always, though, other voices are here to affirm that Disney does, in fact, create transcendence, the letting go of reality for a fantasy that, for a time, feels even more real. So that, whether you're watching a Disney movie, listening to a Disney song, reading a Disney book, going on a Disney attraction or cruise, or more, these more eternal things are also being engraved on you. Something that doesn't only entertain but sustains, something noticed by Dave Snell and Jody Maberry.

"I have always felt a connection with Disney," said Dave Snell, long-time Disney fan, cybersecurity consultant, and owner of the Snell Advisory Group. "My dad was in the Navy, so I moved around a lot as a kid. Then, I followed in my father's footsteps and joined the Navy, and moved around a lot, too. Through all those moves there was one constant—Disney movies and cartoons, which allowed me continuity and some escape from life.

"Along the way, I first made it to Disney World in college. While there, I quickly realized that it was more innocent, that it was a place where you could be yourself and use your imagination. Like Disney movies while I was a kid, the visit impacted me in realizing it was a place where someone was allowed to escape from reality—not a bad thing when, as a kid, I couldn't talk to my dad for months at a time when he deployed on submarines, or later, as an adult, when I was caught up in the realities of deployments myself.

"Flashing forward, in 2011, after returning from a deployment in Afghanistan, we brought our daughter to Disney World for her third birthday. The look on her face when she saw the arch announcing our arrival is indelibly etched in my memory. Then in 2018, my daughter's dance company went down to Disney World for an exposition. It is experiences like these that make memories and add to the enjoyment that I have associated with Disney parks.

"Of course, I have hundreds of other memories from which to choose in which my family and I were able to tap into our imaginations, to think and feel in a place where things are more innocent. I have been so thrilled to share my love of Disney movies, cartoons, and parks with my family. Now, at this stage in my life, I hope to work for Disney. To be part of a place that keeps the wonder and innocence alive in all of us and pass similar memories on to other families."

"My road to working with Disney started with my podcast for park rangers at the country's national parks, along with others—something important to me as a former park ranger. Then I produced an episode about what national parks could learn from Disney's theme parks and vice versa," said Jody Maberry, business and podcast consultant, speaker, coach, and co-host of the *Creating Disney Magic* podcast.

"So, not knowing exactly where to find a guest, I contacted Lee Cockerell, former executive vice president of operations for Walt Disney World after seeing his book, *Creating Magic*." (Author's note: Lee is the father of Dan Cockerell, former vice president of EPCOT, the Magic Kingdom, and Hollywood Studios, who appears in this book.)

"I knew it was a long shot—especially since my podcast was about park rangers, but fortunately, it turned out that Lee's sister-in-law had been a park ranger, too, and before retirement had actually been superintendent of Glacier Bay National Park and Preserve in Alaska. *That* is why I always ask. Because you never know where connections and coincidences can lead—including Lee and myself now co-hosting the *Creating Disney Magic* podcast together.

"One of the things that most draws me to Disney is how much they care about their guests. In fact, I felt that caring the first time I rode *Flight of Passage*. It never crossed my mind that I could ride something that felt real and affected every one of my senses. I really felt like I was on Pandora. And for me, that shows the power of Disney and the Imagineers. Because looking back at that moment, I know that Joe Rohde, the former Imagineer who oversaw creative on Pandora at Animal Kingdom and, in fact, all of the park, wanted guests to really care about Pandora.

"So now I'm in this unique position of being at the center of all these people connected to Disney. Though I've never worked there, I get the benefit of learning all their different stories and philosophies. But at the same time, to best feel the magic that Disney offers, I only need to look closer to home.

"Like when I stood with my daughter in EPCOT, waiting for her to meet the Anna and Elsa characters. My daughter was wearing braids, just like Anna. Well, when she finally got to the front, Elsa told her how Anna uses slobber from Sven the Reindeer to keep her braids in place! That little extra something made my daughter feel like she was in on a secret. And made her feel special."

Yes, it's clear that, in Dave's and Jody's experience, Disney had achieved its goal of sharing feelings of wonder and magic. Especially as both stories center on parents experiencing moments of transcendence with their children.

Walt and his daughters at the carousel?

So, just for good measure, is there any better way to end our chapter on transcendence—before we move on to talking about how you can apply how Disney does that to your own work, home, and life—by showing how, even out in the ocean, on the way to Alaska, a little boy (and by extension, his family) can experience Disney wonder in the form of two words:

"He's here!"

"I believe Disney creates an emotional connection with us by creating something relatable, not only from person to person, but from generation to generation, and country to country. You could probably go anywhere in the world and say 'Mickey Mouse,' and everyone would know who you're talking about," said William Hickey, long-time Disney fan, columnist for *The News & Reporter*, and recruitment relationship manager.

"In fact, it was Mickey's appearance on a Disney cruise that really opened my eyes to what Disney means. In 2019, we arranged a Disney cruise trip for our whole family to Alaska. The moment that most comes to mind happened on the first night on the ship. We had all gathered for dinner—my wife, my parents, my sisters and their significant others, everyone, including my three nephews.

"After dinner, as dessert was being served, the staff all started coming out into the dining room, and suddenly Mickey appeared...and, at that moment, my 3-year-old nephew stood up and pointed, so excited he could barely get the words out. So, he's pointing, and he shouted, 'He's here! He's here!' Then he turned to my mother and loudly said, 'I didn't know *he'd* be here!' and he's just beside himself. And at that moment, my mother turned back to us, and I could see she was starting to well up.

"Later, she said, 'With everything it took to get everyone here, all the time, the cost, the scheduling...that makes it worth it.'

"I think Disney creates that emotional connection because they have managed to hook on to something that we can all relate to, and that was very apparent in my nephew that day. And it's one of those things I will always remember."

Questions

1. Looking back, have you experienced wonder with Disney? If so, how did it feel?

2. Have you experienced "commonly uncommon customer service" with Disney? Like a Cast Member doing something that saved the day—or your vacation—for you or your family?

3. Have you ever noticed how the lighting at a Disney park, including the famous flickering lights, or the color in a Disney movie, made you feel?

4. Is there a specific attraction you've gone on that you'd like to talk about with an Imagineer or Cast Member who worked on it? What would you ask or say?

5. How do you feel when you see the castle or Mickey Mouse for the first time on a Disney trip?

8   How You Can Do That, Too

"In order to make good in your chosen task, it's important to have someone you want to do it for. The greatest moments in life are not concerned with selfish achievements, but rather with the things we do for the people we love and esteem, and whose respect we need."

Walt Disney

W hew.

Well, it's been quite a journey, hasn't it, from the Table of Contents right up to now? And though I don't foresee having just one answer to our question of how Disney does that by the end of the book, I do believe all the answers will eventually circle back to one.

More on that later.

And though, up until now, I've been starting these chapters by sharing a personal story, I want to now flip that. So, let's talk about *you*.

Yep, you.

Because when we're done here, I want *you* to be able to walk away not only having a better idea of how Disney does that, but how you can, too. Causing ripples, leaving people you interact with at work and home and everywhere in between asking themselves, "How does (insert your name) do that?"

At work, for example, they'll ask questions like, "How do they always get so much out of their team?" And "How is it that, no matter what challenges come up, they still somehow bring projects in on time and under budget?" Also "Why do the customers seem to love all the new things they introduce?"

At home, the questions will sound slightly different, but will still, in the end, touch on the same themes. Like "How do they make me feel so good about being with them?" and "How do they manage to always make our family feel like the most important thing in their lives?" And "How did they help our kids believe that they should follow their passion?"

And aren't those the types of questions we all want to leave in our wake? Making other people feel the way Disney makes us feel.

Well, thankfully now that we've seen more of how Disney does that, we can apply the same principles in our lives.

So, where to start?

Well, to quote seven hard-working miners we know, "Heigh-ho, heigh-ho, it's off to work we go."

At work

Before we begin, I'd like you to take a test. Now, don't worry, you don't have to fill in little circles with your razor-sharp No. 2 pencil. All you need to do is take a few minutes to answer these Maslow-inspired questions about your work (now, when I say "work," it can be whatever that means in your life):

- Does your organization create strong emotional connections with people?

- Does your organization have an enduring, compelling vision?

- Does your organization make people feel like they're part of something bigger?

- Does your organization help people play, follow their passion, and find their path?

- Does your organization help people experience wonder?

Ok, yes, so I know it will take a bit of time to answer these, but the cool thing is that you don't have to answer them all at once. No, the point really is to just stay aware of the questions as much as you can throughout your day—and then see if your answers change as you apply, or inspire others to apply, the Disney lessons you've learned in this book to your organization. Because, in the end, if your organization treats people like they matter—your customers, colleagues, partners, investors, funders, and others alike—they'll keep coming back.

Does your organization create strong emotional connections with people?

This is a tricky section. Because it might seem like I'm saying you should create emotional connections because it's good for business.

And that's because I am.

Huh?

Here's the thing. I am not saying you should create emotional connections only because it's good for business. No, I personally believe that the primary reason we should do it is because people generally deserve to be treated that way. And how does it feel to be treated like that? Where your needs are front and center (and I mean really centered, like using

Ctrl+E on your keyboard in Microsoft Word...go ahead, I'll wait while you try it).

Well, to know how it feels to be treated in such a way that an emotional connection is made, just ask the person closest to you.

You.

If an organization treats you like they care about your needs, how might you feel? And, over time, if you continue to be treated that way, what might that help you believe about the organization, and yourself, and how might that make you act? And how might your actions help others? And then, if a byproduct of that feeling is that you engage more with the organization, and enough people do the same, and the organization grows and can help more people, isn't that a good thing? Get it? Primary reason: because you deserve care. Secondary reason: more business success for the organization.

As always, though, let's bring in other voices to confirm this approach, including a former Disney executive, two long-time Disney fans, and our good friend, Mr. Skees.

"Storytelling creates emotional connections and emotional connections create more engagement. For guests and Cast Members, this means more personal connections and memories. And, for the business world, more engagement turns into more brand loyalty, which means people are much more likely to come back again, which then creates even more of an emotional connection," explains Dan Cockerell, author, consultant, and former vice president of Disney's EPCOT, Hollywood Studios, and Magic Kingdom parks.

"My personal experience with Disney started when, as a teenager, my family drove to Disney World from New York. Then my wife, Denise, and I went there for our first anniversary," said Lawrence Sprung, founder of Mitlin Financial Inc., podcast host of *Mitlin Money Mindset™*, author of *Financial Planning Made Personal*, and an Adventures by Disney Insider. "After that, we began visiting regularly, bringing our boys, too.

"When did I know I was hooked? When my wife booked a Disney cruise for our tenth wedding anniversary in November 2010. Now, I had never been a 'cruise-type-of-guy,' but I reluctantly agreed as she made a good case about it being something the boys would enjoy and where we could also get some 'alone time.' After just one day on the ship, I went to the desk and waited in a fairly long line to book our next cruise. And, even better, I got a discount for booking it onboard!

"Then one night during the cruise, my wife and I went for our own special dinner, while our young kids hung out with the Disney camp groups for their ages. The boys had so much fun that when I went to pick them up, they didn't want to leave. Now that makes for very happy parents, alone time with no guilt!

"I genuinely enjoyed the cruise and our kids enjoyed hanging out with us. We've also had these same types of experiences at the Disney parks and with the Adventures by Disney program, which—in my eyes—takes Disney's customer service to a whole other level. I think so much of that has to do with the Disney Cast Members. Everything they do is done with sincerity, which is important to me. The level of connection they build with guests fosters good relationships.

"As a business owner, I understand good relationships are good for business. But relationships cannot be built with an effort to 'get something out of it.' They need to be genuine and with an effort to make a connection. The Disney Cast Members we have encountered during our travels have made those connections with my family. This is why Disney makes us feel so special. We know it's a business. But at the same time, they make us feel like family."

"We first went to Disney World in February 1972, and my parents took us back regularly. In fact, I became such a Disney fan that, when I attended the University of Illinois, all my friends would go to Daytona Beach or Fort Lauderdale for spring break, but I'd have them drop me at Disney World!" said Doug Rabold, long-time Disney fan, CX portfolio manager, and consultant.

"Those trips, coupled with my love of Disney and its commitment to quality service, have very much informed my career. For example, as the director of an IT global service desk, I trained our agents to look at everything through an experience lens, not just a typical help desk transaction.

"I did that by first asking them, 'What's the difference between customer service and customer experience?' My answer: It's easy to provide good service on one activity, but much harder to deliver an exceptional overall experience. That's because there are many different touchpoints along the customer journey to build upon that sentiment.

"How do I know what that kind of exceptional experience looks and feels like? Because I have seen it with Disney for so many years. I've also been writing about it for a long time, too, in my Disney *Magic Moments* articles on LinkedIn.

"One of the examples I share with my trainees to illustrate the kind of experience Disney creates relates to the fact that I live in Texas, just two highway exits away from a large regional theme park for which I have had an annual pass for many years. We also have annual passes to Disney World.

"After sharing that, I ask them how often they think I've visited that regional park in the past year. After all, I explain, it's easy to hop in my car and drive there in a few minutes. Then I ask them how often they think I've gone to Disney World in that same period. And, of course, with Disney World, it's not nearly so easy. I have to make hotel and flight reservations, board an airplane, stay at a hotel, and so on.

"The answer? I went to the regional theme park one time in the last year, while I went to Disney World four times! And, when I do go to the regional park, though it's fun, I often walk out thinking about how much I spent and when will my kids make me go back next. Contrast that to the last day of my Disney visits when I'm already planning the next trip."

Theron's Keys #8: Creating magic creates business

Disney tells optimistic stories in a sophisticated way. This then emotionally connects guests to the stories to the point where they want to experience them again and again. So, although it's a recipe for creating wonder, it's also an effective business strategy.

To make this happen, it's better to think about customers as "audience members." And then your product or service becomes an "experience" for them. Of course, an "experience" is made up of many dynamic elements, and if those elements are not maintained or start to fail, the perceived value of the experience really degrades.

For example, if you want people to feel safe, happy, and comfortable in your venue, you don't want to have trash overflowing in receptacles, broken handles on doors, and rude staff; this definitely doesn't feel safe or comfortable and guests won't be happy. Because when too many elements go wrong, it erodes the experience and takes people right out of the story and place, so that they're no longer able to suspend their disbelief.

But when you get it right, you then turn your product or service, including a theme park attraction, into something much more. As it happened for James on *Flight of Passage* where he could physically feel the drop into Pandora, see and hear the animals running, feel the wind and breeze of the sea on his face, smell the salt water, and feel his banshee breathing beneath him.

As a result, he could totally forget that he was on an attraction and accept that he was in an impossibly spectacular fantasy world that he one hundred percent fully perceived as real. And *that's* magic. That's the emotional connection. That's the moment orchestrated to create that emotional bond. And that was the most exciting part of what we did as Imagineers, and what experience design teams do all over the world!

Remember, Walt didn't just create movies, stories, characters, and theme parks. He created an optimistic world of experiences. What if we did the same? And, at work and home, express the idea of "What can we do today to help create someone's 'Happily Ever After?'"

Does your organization have an enduring, compelling vision?

Do you cringe when you hear the word "vision"? If so, you may be one of those veterans of grueling corporate "vision statement" development sessions, where twenty-three people gather in a board room with lower-tier snacks and brainstorm every word that should be used, including "leverage," "synergize," and "solutions."

Well, if that describes your experience, then please understand two things. First, that my day job has been in communications and marketing for over twenty-five years, so I've been in my fair share of those types of sessions. And second, that when I say "vision" here, I'm really referring to two of the definitions of the word (as a noun) by Merriam-Webster:

"Manifestation to the senses of something immaterial"
"Thought, concept, or object formed by the imagination"

Sound familiar? Like the work of any mustachioed visionary you know?

For me, I can feel the power of Walt's vision—his ability to imagine what wasn't yet there and manifest it—every time I walk through a Disney park, watch a Disney movie, hear a Disney song, and so on and so on. When I talk to people who have worked for Disney, who have been entrusted with keeping that vision alive, it literally seems to burn through them.

And of course, all of that is still happening even though, as of the writing of this book, Walt has been gone for over fifty-seven years.

That's enduring.

Which also makes me think about what it must have been like when Walt shared his vision with his team, or others, like bankers and distributors. How animated (pun definitely intended) he must have been in that moment and, by extension, how that would then likely animate them. To the point that they were willing and able to do things they probably didn't believe they could do at first—or maybe even wanted to. Fueled by his passion and belief until it became their own. Like on the night he acted out *Snow White and the Seven Dwarfs* for his entire studio. After all, in that moment, he was asking his team to do something that no one had ever done or thought could be or should be done, and, ultimately, to believe that animation could actually make people feel, not just laugh.

Then, imagine what that might have looked and felt like if you had been sitting there. With Walt sharing his vision for the film directly with you and your colleagues. Imagine his eyes as the story came to life, literally with every word. Imagine the cadence of those words. The confidence with which they were being delivered. The voices of the different characters he assumed in those moments, rising and falling dramatically, as his body also magically took on their forms. His animated facial expressions and theatrical hand gestures. All driven by the force of his personality and passion.

How might have you reacted sitting in that audience? Would his passion have become yours? His belief? His "need to make it happen"? Would your legs have bounced up and down nervously as he continued, with the excitement building to get back to your office and begin sketching and storyboarding? Dare I say, without a doubt.

That's compelling.

So, let's now turn back to you. Does your organization have a vision that would inspire that kind of passion? If not, get a few people in a room (not too many, and make sure they're from different levels of the organization, not just executives—maybe a customer and supplier, too—and oh yeah, try to avoid clichés and get some good snacks).

Then everyone works on answering this one question: In the future, when our organization is effortlessly doing what it was created to do, what will that look, sound, and feel like on a typical day, for our customers, employees, partners, and community? What would make them experience wonder?

Then start writing.

After that, if your statement passes the goosebumps test, then make sure everyone in the organization knows it, understands how to implement it through your mission, and can say it in their sleep, or at least while lightly dozing. But don't worry about putting it on glass cubes on everyone's desk. Just make it sincere. And spread it organically.

Most important, ask every leader to model it and look for behaviors that support it and those that don't. If the behaviors don't, your leaders should coach quietly. If the behaviors do, they can recognize loudly.

Then don't change your vision. Ever. Unless you absolutely have to.

Because a vision that keeps changing...isn't one.

Be like Walt.

"I remember being six, crowding around the TV on Sunday nights with my family to watch the Disney show," said John Pogachar, long-time Disney fan, author of *Mom & Dad: Ten Things I Want You to Know Before I'm One Week Old!*, life coach, and founder of the Love on Every Billboard international movement. "During it, Disney would open a book and talk about a fairy tale that his team had brought to life. Then one day, the show was in color! I just remember being excited about his creativity. He was this really cool creator with an amazing imagination.

"I didn't get to Disneyland until I was 21, but it was wonderful to see it myself and through the eyes of my children. There was so much wonder everywhere. We all ran for the rides. That day I felt like I'd turned back into that little kid who always wanted to go but didn't have the chance.

"Walt was so good at showing people what he wanted, and then having them carry that to others. To get any money at all, he had to inspire investors and bankers; he had to paint this vision, for them to be *there* and see it. Even when someone told him no, he just kept doing it.

"And with Walt doing what he did, I'm sure it inspired others to do something, too. He paved the way for any kind of amusement park. Now there are so many other parks. Then came Disney World, the Disney Cruise Line, and more.

"He brought that vision to life. He had it inside of him, then lived from that vision. He had worked on his mindset for so long, to not have fear or, if he did, to not let it stop him. Then he painted the picture so bright, so real, that his people created what he saw. Like President Kennedy setting a vision for the space program to get to the moon.

"We usually say, you have to see it to believe it. But with Walt, he believed it and then saw it. Believed it to the point that he could touch it, saw the full-length animated film even before they began, the buildings going up at Disneyland before construction started, all of it. And he got others to do the same."

Disney's movie *The Santa Clause*, released in 1994, spoke to the power of vision to magically create reality, with quite a few jokes along the way, of course. In the scene where Judy the Elf explains to Scott Calvin (the new Santa Claus) that magic is real, she says, "Seeing isn't believing, believing is seeing." If Walt were there, he likely wouldn't have needed the explanation.

Does your organization make people feel like they're part of something bigger?

Does your organization bring people together, either directly because of their own efforts or indirectly because of how people feel about it? Obviously, Disney does both, directly through its offerings and service, and indirectly, by inspiring a huge global following of fan groups and sites, influencers, events, associated businesses, and a variety of additional partners and independent projects, which were born out of a love of Disney (like this book).

In the same way, does *your* organization bring people together directly because of its offerings and service? And indirectly, by inspiring your customers to show their loyalty in a variety of ways, including through fan groups and sites, meetups, and conventions? And, maybe even one day, when the time and tide is just right, by inspiring one of your customers to write a book like this about your organization?

Want to know just how powerful that indirect impact can be, where people come together because of their love for an organization? For that, we can look at the phenomenal growth that Skip Sher has experienced with his Disney Day Drinkers Club group on Facebook.

Wait, what, why are we talking about drinking in a Disney book?!

Well, for several reasons.

But before we get to them, let me be perfectly, completely, crystally clear. We're talking about drinking in a respectful way that fits within the positive family atmosphere that Disney encourages.

Ok, now let's talk about those reasons.

First, Disney itself obviously recognizes how cocktails, and other alcoholic beverages, fit within the overall adult experience of their parks, resorts, cruises, events, and other offerings. Look no further than the International Food & Wine Festival specifically, and the World Showcase, in general, at EPCOT. Or to the many places at the other Disney parks and resorts around the world, on the cruise line, and at other Disney venues, where adults can drink.

My wife, Gina, a mixologist who got 100% on her bartending school exam (and yes, she won't be pleased with my bragging about her here), explained to me how cocktails can actually be an immersive experience themselves, especially with Disney. And, as you read her words, notice how much the focus areas she talks about could apply to an attraction:

"With Disney, it starts with the environment of where you're having the cocktail, like at one of their bars or lounges," Gina began. "Is it meant to be warm and cozy, romantic, or lively and upbeat? And does the lighting and other theming reflect that? For example, at Disney World, the *Barcelona Lounge* at Disney's Coronado Springs Resort is modern, bright, and welcoming; *Geyser Point Bar & Grill* at Disney's Wilderness Resort makes me feel like I'm in another part of the world; and the *Enchanted Rose* at the Grand Floridian is dark, mysterious, and romantic.

"Next, the bartender plays an important role. If they are fun, make you feel valued, listen to what you want, and are confident enough to help you figure out what you want even when you don't know what you want, then that can really make the experience. And I have to say that Disney bartenders are consistently fun and knowledgeable and provide excellent service.

"Then comes the drink itself. First, seeing it, whether it's the glistening ice or condensation, a coated rim, the garnish. Also, what it comes in, whether it's a copper mug or frosted martini glass. When done right, just the sight of the drink should be enticing and aesthetically pleasing.

"Then comes smelling and tasting it. Even before you take a sip, you can take in its aroma, smelling the different spirits, the lemon or lime wedge, cinnamon sticks, and so on. You often know right in those first few seconds how you feel about the drink. But then that first sip can evolve. And over time, as ice melts, garnishes infuse, and more, it can become a completely different drink, a different experience.

"To really understand how memorable the experience can be, I just have to think back to the first time we ate as a family at *Chefs de France* in EPCOT. I ordered a Kir Royale, and it was amazing. I had never had it before, and the fact that I was having it at Disney with my family made it even more special. I remember that Disney memory now like it happened last week.

"Disney also does a nice job of matching the atmosphere and environment with the drink. For example, you wouldn't want to be offered a Kir Royale at *La Cava del Tequila* in the Mexico Pavilion. It would be like someone was suddenly shaking you, waking you up, and removing you from the experience.

"As to bringing everyone together, we have met so many wonderful people at Disney through cocktail experiences. We've also met many more through Skip Sher's group. I even reconnected with someone from grade school in it!"

Second, as Gina mentions, some of the nicest Cast Members we have met at Disney include the bartenders and bartending staff.

And third, the primary thing that binds the people in Skip's group together is a love of Disney, as you'll hear about in his story. They just happen to focus on another way Disney does that.

So, how powerfully and quickly does Disney inspire people to come together in different ways? Well, all you need to know is that, as of the writing of this book, and a little over two years after the launch of Skip's group, they now have over 100,000 members (and I literally must keep checking back every week or so as this book nears the publishing date to update that to the next thousand).

"My parents took me as a kid to Disney World, and I loved EPCOT. I also come from that generation where, even though Walt wasn't alive when I was growing up, you'd see Disney in a lot of places, including on Sunday night television with *Walt Disney's Wonderful World of Color* and its different versions. As a kid, seeing that, I couldn't wait to go. And, as a kid, when you got there it definitely didn't disappoint," said Skip Sher, founder of the Disney Day Drinkers Club Group on Facebook, and account executive for a multi-platform audio content and entertainment company.

"Now, a lot of people, once they become teenagers or young adults, want to recapture that innocence of childhood. I know I did. So as soon as I turned 18, I realized that I didn't have to wait for my parents to take me. I could go whenever I wished. Then when you turn 21, you get to do one extra thing you couldn't do before at a Disney park: have a drink. Of course, cocktails have always been part of Disney—including at *Club 33*, in the resorts, and so on.

"In founding the Disney Day Drinkers Club on Facebook, I wanted to make sure that our group was useful for someone coming to Disney for the first time or the twentieth time! Plus, I think people really enjoy the social aspects of the group, like attending meetups in the parks, and just being able to talk and share pictures with others who love Disney like they do. That's because our group is primarily made up of people who love and understand Disney first and then cocktails second. It's that love of Disney that binds us.

"As a Disney adult, of course, I know it's perfectly fine to have some cocktails, but as a club, we never encourage, or want to see, anyone at a Disney park drinking too much, sneaking drinks into the park, and so on. It's all about being respectful and practicing moderation. This also ensures that anyone who is having drinks doesn't intrude on anyone's vacation or special moments. We also work hard to make sure that the group stays a positive, respectful place.

"One last thing I want to mention: the Disney bartenders. What makes them special, besides being great people, is that they are often the one type of Cast Member you can really spend time with and get to know, since you're typically just walking past a ride operator, for example. I consider them to be the best bartenders in the world. Plus, they're at Disney, that thing we all loved as kids. And so, everything and everyone associated with Disney just seems to have that magic."

Author's note: The Disney Day Drinkers Club supports several charities, including Give Kids The World Village®.

Does your organization help people play, follow their passion, and find their path?

When's the last time you played at work? I mean, besides when the meeting organizers put a Slinky and Play-Doh in the middle of the tables at your recent workshop to get everyone thinking creatively?

When was the last time you were able to learn a new skill you always wanted to try, or think outside the box on a new process, without worrying at first whether it was feasible, how much it would cost, or how long it would take to implement? And when I say, "outside the box," I mean outside the box of the roles we either get put into or put ourselves into way too often as we grow up. Confined by past experience and limited by cautious expectation.

Do you remember *playing*?

If you need some help remembering, I'll give you a few clues as to tendencies you'll see and feel when people are playing, following their passion, and finding their path. They smile and laugh more often. They compete less and collaborate more. They do better work because they're enthusiastic. Their days fly by. And overall, the customer feels it, because the new product or service developed carries the same energy that was put into it. Like the Imagineers' passion I felt on *Flight of Passage*.

Is it important to play? Yes, indeed. Because to be able to really play, we must let go of everything else for a while. The worries. The "To Do" and "Right Now!" lists. The past stories about how it couldn't be done. And to, instead, become child-like again. Which then helps us get back in touch with our passion, the thing we love to do no matter who's watching, who's paying us, if at all, and how much time is left on the clock. And of course, when we put our talents and passions together in a way that serves others, that then can illuminate a future path for us—or re-illuminate one that somehow got lost in the shadows.

As always, to see this in action as it applies to Disney, let's watch as a master woodcarver follows his path from playing drums to creating signs for Disney; a former Disney Cast Member brings together his love of Disney, video games, and Legos to serve so many at such an important time; and a former Imagineer transfers the love of what he does to guests through shows and attractions.

"I started playing drums when I was younger. But then my dad told me I should have a backup career, so I started playing the bass!" said Ray Kinman, independent Disney artist and master woodcarver. "After that, I took up woodcarving and started creating signs.

"When my kids were very young, we did what many parents do: took our children to Disneyland for an adventure! I had been carving professionally for several years already, so while we were there, I looked around and thought, 'You know, I think that I can probably do stuff like this.' So, I found the Disney Imagineering address and sent a letter to the graphic design department—many, many times. After not hearing back, though, I stopped trying, which incidentally is a big mistake. Your greatest asset isn't your education or your connections or how smart you are or even the quality of your work. Your greatest asset is your persistence...I was young at the time, and it took me awhile to learn that.

"Then one day, I got a call from a senior graphic designer at Disney Imagineering who just happened to wander into a restaurant where I had done some signage and got my number from the manager. He asked me to submit more examples of my work. About a week after I sent them, he called back, saying they had a project they'd like me to look at and asked if I could come in and present my portfolio to the Imagineers. I said 'yes' right away.

"When I arrived, I was escorted to a board room with about a dozen Imagineers gathered around a large meeting table. Needless to say, I was really nervous, sitting there with some of the best artists and creative minds in the world.

"I had brought photos of my pieces and circulated them around the table. They then interviewed me with some direct questions. I guess I did okay because somebody then brought out rolled up blueprints for me to look at. I figured they would give me some obscure little project... something to test me on, right? But when I unrolled the blueprints, I immediately swallowed hard. They were starting me at the very top...the *Indiana Jones Adventure* project.

"After talking through technical details and design issues, I stopped and said, 'Look, you guys...I really want this job!' After a moment of silence, the art director looked up at me and a little smile settled on his face as he said, 'Yeah...we can tell!'

"Long story short, I got the gig, the carve went well, and they were pleased. And it started a relationship which has lasted many years. Since then, I've created many signs for Disneyland, California Adventure, and Disney World, including *The Many Adventures of Winnie the Pooh*, *Splash Mountain*, *Country Bear Jamboree*, the *Village Haus Restaurant*, *Fantasyland Theatre*, and many more.

"Here's the deal: at the time, I didn't realize what working with Disney would mean for my career. I thought it was interesting work and the money was good. It was this experience, though, which would eventually allow me, now, as a father of five and grandfather of seven, to do what I have done for all these years—work with wonderful people, teach woodcarving to pass it on to the next generation, and do what I can to bring a little bit of good into the world."

"I have always felt a connection with Disney," said Darren d'Hedouville, former Disney Cast Member with support roles for Walt Disney Imagineering, former gaming development coordinator at Give Kids The World Village®, and founder at MCParks.

"Growing up in New York, my parents took me to Disney World once or twice a year. I also always loved video games and Legos. So I put those passions together in 2013, when my friends and I started a Minecraft project and built Walt Disney World on the platform.

"A few years later I entered the Disney College Program, working in the Attractions department as a host, then moved on to training and became a coordinator. After a few years in Park Operations, I moved to the Polynesian Village Resort at the front desk and then to Magic Kingdom Guest Relations.

"In 2020, though, the pandemic hit and, like so many other things, all the Disney parks began shutting down. And suddenly our Minecraft project became the only place to watch a Disney-style fireworks production each night. This contributed to the growth of the project, and we began to look for nonprofits to support. That's when Give Kids The World Village® came into view—an organization that serves critically ill children and their families.

"Once we toured the Village, saw the amazing things happening, experienced the venues, and met the staff, volunteers, and families, we knew there was something very different about the place. And that's when we knew we wanted to do more than just support the Village with fundraising—but also make more people aware of what a special place it was by building it in Minecraft and virtually opening its gates to everyone.

"In working with the Village, we then realized that the Minecraft platform could become an excellent tool for the families coming there, too. For many of them, though the trip was exciting, it could also be overwhelming, especially while attending to a critically ill child. So we created a virtual version of families' Wish trips. That way, before they came they could figure out what they most wanted to do. Plus, it was often hard emotionally for the families to leave, with many saying it was the best week they'd ever had, so this way they would have a way of looking back.

"After touring the Village and working on the Minecraft project for them, I realized I wanted to be even more involved. So after learning that the Village was looking for a fundraising person who brought video gaming experience, I applied. A few days later, I was offered the role.

"Now of course, I loved my job at Disney, so it was bittersweet to leave. But I see many common threads between Disney and Give Kids The World Village®. And, in many ways, I felt like this was the natural next step, a way to impact people who were managing one of the most difficult things possible."

According to minecraft.net/en-us, "Minecraft is a game made up of blocks, creatures, and community. Blocks can be used to reshape the world or build fantastical creations. Creatures can be battled or befriended, depending on your playstyle. Experience epic adventures solo or with friends..."

"I was four years old when Disneyland opened. Prior to that, we had been watching the Disneyland television shows regularly. One day my father said, 'Ok, we're going to save up and go!' which took us about four years," said Mark Rhodes, former senior show writer, director, and producer at Walt Disney Imagineering, author, and owner, president, and creative lead at Rhodes to Imagination, Inc.

"When we got there, we spent the whole day at the park. My favorite rides were *Peter Pan's Flight* and *Mr. Toad's Wild Ride*. I also remember having a great time on *Tom Sawyer Island* with my younger brother. After that we visited Disneyland every couple of years. Though I never really thought of it as a place where you could work!

"During high school, I published my first novel before going to Colorado State University. At the time, I was performing in theater groups during the summer, then I published another novel. This was also about the time that, as a backup career, my dad encouraged me to attend bartending school, where I graduated.

"Next, my brother and I applied for jobs at Disneyland. He went into finance, and I became a utility man at *Club 33*, a role I soon learned was both a busboy and dishwasher. It was there I worked with Kevin Rafferty, another former Imagineer and now a life-long friend. Then I became a bartender there and was soon serving drinks at the only place at the time anyone could drink at the Magic Kingdom.

"Around that same time, Disney was also working on the Tokyo Disneyland project, and because of my writing background, I was asked to help document the standard operating procedures for all the Disneyland attractions, stores, etc., so that they could use them in the new park.

"That led to me getting transferred to WED Enterprises (precursor to Walt Disney Imagineering), where I was assigned to Project Management to write descriptions of the EPCOT pavilions. I was then transferred to Creative Design and had the great fortune to work with Ward Kimball, Marc Davis, Claude Coats, Jimmy MacDonald, Tony Baxter, Joe Lanzisero, Kevin Rafferty, Joe Rohde, and many other great Imagineers. It was also fantastic working under Marty Sklar and John Hench.

"I then did show writing for an update of *The Enchanted Tiki Room* and scripted the *Alice in Wonderland* attraction at Disneyland. After that, I worked with Joe Rohde on what would become the *Maelstrom* attraction at EPCOT. Then came *Splash Mountain* for Tokyo with Joe Lanzisero and Florida's Magic Kingdom with Don Caron. Kevin Rafferty and I also did scripting for the comedy club at Pleasure Island.

"As you can tell, I've already had quite a ride and continue to do what I love with my own company. When I look back at the common thread that bonded all of us at Disney together, especially the Imagineers, it was having a passion for what we did. We fell in love with what we were doing, and we hoped that love would show up for guests through the shows and attractions we created."

Does your organization help people experience wonder?

Think back to how you imagine my children's faces looked when their grandparents walked into the restaurant at the Grand Floridian, how my daughter looked when I handed her back her purse, how my wife looks every time we drive under the Walt Disney World welcome sign, and how I looked on *Flight of Passage* that day.

Then, as I asked you at the end of the last chapter, think back to moments of wonder you've had with Disney. And, as you do, go look in the mirror.

Yep, that's what wonder looks like.

Next, ask yourself if your organization ever helps people look that way. What products, services, or other offerings do you have, coupled of course with the manner in which you offer them, that could make people feel wonder?

If you don't have any, it's important that you either find some among your existing offerings or create them. Because if you're not causing wonder, you're missing out on two major opportunities. First, to make the world better. And second, to make your organization better...and bigger. And notice what I put first there. Because, as Lawrence Strung explained earlier, if you put business first and people second, your customers will feel that and act—or not act—accordingly.

Now, when I thought about the story that best summed up everything we've talked about in this chapter—emotional connection, compelling vision, feeling part of something bigger, people following their passion, and that all-important sense of wonder—I immediately thought of the one that Pamela Landwirth, president and CEO of Give Kids The World Village®, shared with me.

After you read it, I'm confident you'll know why I did.

"My original plan after graduating from college was to work for Disney for a few months before continuing my education," said Pamela Landwirth, former Disney executive, president and CEO of Give Kids The World Village®, and author of *On Purpose: How Engagement Drives Success*.

"Because of that, I asked to be put in fast foods where I knew high turnover was expected; however, I was cast in a role in Guest Services at the front desk of Disney's Lake Buena Vista Resorts. It was a match made in heaven. I fell in love with the hospitality industry and being able to learn it from the best—Disney!

"I then became an interviewer in Casting. At the time, rather than hire individuals with professional staffing experience, Disney sought out current Cast Members who exhibited the qualities they were looking for in new hires and trained them in interviewing skills. This was a brilliant strategy. The thought was that people would hire in their own image, and that Cast Members with front-line experience also understood first-hand the challenges and opportunities of each role and could better explain the job responsibilities. This was just one of many valuable lessons I learned throughout my Disney career, lessons that would serve me well in my current role.

"At Disney, the number one role Cast Members have is to create happiness for their guests. But Disney knows that if Cast Members aren't happy in their roles, they cannot create happiness for guests. So the philosophy was 'Take care of your cast, they will take care of the guests, and the bottom line will take care of itself.' Now of course, many might think that's common sense, but common sense isn't always common practice.

"I was then thrilled to be able to put what I had learned from my Casting/onboarding experience to good use at Disney when I went back into the field in Resort Operations including stints in Guest Services, Lodging, Housekeeping, Food & Beverage, Reservations, and Human Resources. I even got to 'Cross-U' in Attractions and Entertainment in the parks.

"I also served on the pre-opening teams for many of the Disney hotels and spent several months in Paris on the Euro Disney pre-opening team. I had the opportunity to teach 'Disney Traditions' and many other programs. I never turned down an opportunity to grow and learn more about the Disney organization and the hospitality/theme park industry. Little did I realize at the time that each one of these opportunities and learning experiences was preparing me for my current role at Give Kids The World.

"Soon after returning home from Paris, I met and later married Henri Landwirth, the founder of Give Kids The World Village® for critically ill children and their families from around the world who wish to experience all the magic Central Florida has to offer...and they often wish to go to Disney!

"One of my favorite quotes is, 'The meaning of life is to find your gift, the purpose of life is to give it away.' As I became more engaged in the Village, I realized that as much as I loved Disney, I knew it was time to take all the great experience I had gained there and bring it to helping the critically ill children and their families being served at the Village.

"The similarities between the two organizations are striking. Both are dedicated to creating happiness, life-long memories, and the perfect guest experience. Disney wants to create that experience so their guests will return time and time again. At the Village, we want to create the perfect guest experience because our guests cannot return. Each child is given only one wish trip, so we have only one opportunity to create that perfect guest experience. For one week, we do everything in our power to give our precious guests everything from life's simplest pleasures to the stuff that dreams are made of.

"When critically ill children from around the world are given one wish, half of them choose to visit Walt Disney World. They want to meet Mickey Mouse. They want to meet their favorite princesses. They want to experience first-hand the magic they see through movies, books, and television.

"To give more background on the Village, Henri Landwirth, against all odds, embodied childlike wonder, curiosity, and innovation. Those odds included spending five years in concentration camps as a child and losing most of his family during the Holocaust. Then, after coming to America, through a series of serendipitous events, he came to own the first Holiday Inn right outside the main gate of Disney World. Because of that location, he would get calls from wish-granting organizations, asking if he would provide complimentary accommodations for the wish children and their families. He would always say yes.

"Then one day, he learned that for one little girl, time simply ran out and she lost her battle against leukemia before her wish could be granted. At that point, rather than rest on the laurels of having impacted countless families, he was curious.

"He asked questions and did research. And in doing so, he found that it could take several months to fulfill a wish because of the complexity of the logistics involved. He believed he could streamline the process and bring families to Central Florida in less than 24 hours if need be. So he met with key folks at Disney, and they committed on the spot to helping make it happen. Then he went to SeaWorld, and they did the same. And on and on.

"He promised that no child's wish to come to Central Florida would go unfulfilled. And he did that when he was sixty, an age at which most people with his level of success and history would be thinking of retirement. Rather than being bitter about what he had experienced during the Holocaust, Henri felt he was spared for a reason, and Give Kids The World became the embodiment of his driving force to give back, to make a difference in the lives of children.

"Give Kids The World was founded in 1986 in a storeroom of his Holiday Inn. A few years later, as the need continued to grow, Henri started building the Village in Kissimmee. It opened with fifteen acres and sixteen two-bedroom, two-bath wheelchair accessible villas—and has since grown to eighty-nine acres with 166 villas, four wheelchair-accessible rides, a boundless playground, a miniature golf course, a zero-entry resort pool, an ice cream shop open all day, every day, and surprises around every corner.

"Since opening, we've fulfilled Henri's promise to not turn away any child between the ages of three and eighteen whose wish is to come here. The power of that promise is that we've had the privilege of welcoming nearly 200,000 critically ill children and their families from around the world. We provide accommodations, theme park tickets, meals, daily gifts, and entertainment offerings morning and evening. We celebrate holidays every day, too! Families also get to go to all the area theme parks and receive VIP treatment!

"To really understand the experience the Village offers, think of the happiest day of your life: the day you got married, had your first child, or welcomed your first grandchild. You were on top of the world. That's the feeling we try to create for the families we serve. The seven days spent at the Village are often the happiest days of their lives. It's a time to reconnect as a family. There is nothing here to remind them of the world they have become accustomed to since their child's diagnosis...

doctor's visits, hospital stays, and medical treatments. Here everything revolves around childlike wonder. Our mission is to create the happiness that inspires hope.

"So many families with critically ill children feel alone. They sometimes lose friends because people can't relate to what they're going through. But when, as part of their time here, these families go in and see the personalized stars of every wish child who has visited the Village adorning the ceiling of our Castle of Miracles, they don't feel alone anymore. It gives them a sense of belonging. They feel normal.

"We call our staff Storytellers because they become engaged in the stories the families create at the Village. Of course, yes, we've lost many children whom we got close to during their visits. In those moments, we try to reflect on the happiness we provided them when they were here and the cherished memories we created for their families.

"For me, as a leader in the organization, I need to focus on finding that perfect balance between taking care of business and taking care of hearts. For our Storytellers, it is not just a job. We're a family, completely invested in our mission. Here are the guiding principles I share for our leaders:

- Stay focused on our vision and mission.
- Realize that success comes from taking care of business and taking care of hearts.
- Inspect what you expect.
- Focus on the ants...the little things that make a big difference.
- Never underestimate the power of even the smallest random act of kindness.
- Embrace childlike wonder!
- People will always remember how you made them feel.

"Looking at our ongoing partnership with Disney, I know that people of all ages just love all things Disney. They return time and again because of the feeling they get when they get there...the emotional connection is almost indescribable. It's the ability to step into a place and story where you can forget about everything going on in the 'outside world,' forget all the headlines and all the news, and just live in the moment.

"My father always used to say, 'The world would be a much better place if everyone were more childlike—not childish, mind you—but childlike.' And really, wouldn't the world be a much better place if people were more childlike: being excited, seeing more wonder in simple things, always looking for bright, colorful surprises around every corner, and being willing to try new things?

"Disney and Give Kids The World are both places where people can experience childlike wonder all over again."

According to d23.com, Disney's Cross-Utilization Program, known as "Cross-U," was initiated at Walt Disney World. In the program, office, clerical, and management Cast Members were trained to work as food service and operations hosts/hostesses in the parks during peak holiday periods when high attendance was expected.

On a side note, as I was preparing to write this book, Darren d'Hedouville, who we heard from earlier, gave me a tour of Give Kids The World Village®. When I walked into the Castle of Miracles that Pamela Landwirth referred to above and looked up to see all the personalized stars of the children who had visited the Village, I felt many things.

The first and last was wonder.

At home

Ok, now that we've talked about applying Disney's principles at work, let's see how we can do the same at home (and, again, when I say "home," it can be whatever makes most sense for you, as home can take many forms), using slightly adjusted versions of the questions:

- Do you create strong emotional connections at home?

- Is there a compelling, enduring vision for your home?

- Do you help people in your home feel like they're part of something bigger?

- Do the people in your home feel comfortable enough to play, follow their passion, and find their path?

- Do you help people at home experience wonder?

Unlike before, we won't now look for others to share their stories to expand on these questions. That's because, as you'd imagine, that's for you to do, along with anyone else who comes to mind when you think of "home." But, like before, don't worry about answering them all right away, or in detail. Instead, use them as guideposts, pointing you to creating a home where you can all share your stories and where everyone will, indeed, want to also keep coming back.

In life

I mentioned earlier in the book that Theron and I offered our first *How Does Disney Do That?* presentation last year at EPCOT. Interestingly, it was also the first time we actually met in person after working together remotely for over two years (yeah, I know, a little odd, but "a little odd" sums up a lot of cool coincidences throughout history, doesn't it?).

Near the end of the presentation, Theron shared his thoughts with the audience on applying how Disney does that throughout our lives. Here's pretty much what he said:

"It's important to recognize that every place you go, every experience you have, there's more behind that experience than you might think at first. For example, people always ask me how I stay inspired so that I can also inspire the teams I lead. One way I do that is by recognizing and appreciating the sunrise on my way to work. Seeking things like the beauty of nature allows our mind the time to recognize something truly unique and transformational, and then allow that experience to inspire us.

"But the key is, to be truly inspired, we have to look. Recognizing the beauty in the world and being inspired by it...like noticing how a parent loves their child.

"We can also take that approach when we communicate with someone. Paying attention to them, remembering details about them, making sure it's not just a transactional exchange. That really helps us be part of the solution, not the problem."

For me, what was especially fascinating about what Theron shared that evening at EPCOT was that, with his words, he basically echoed what I had written about in my first book, *Where Are We Going So Fast?: Finding the Sacred in Everyday Moments.*

Now, from previous conversations and practice run-throughs of our presentation, I already knew that Theron wasn't thinking about my first book when he originally came up with the idea of what he'd say. But I didn't fully comprehend until the actual moment he shared his thoughts with the group how perfectly they connected back. Quite a coincidence, wouldn't you say?

But, as I'm guessing you well know by now, to me coincidences mean something. And this coincidence made me realize that, though I never envisioned it, this book is actually a natural extension of my first one.

And once again, it confirmed for me that something bigger brought me and Theron together, especially since we see the world and what's behind it in a similar way. And that this ongoing conversation he and I are having is important—and is one we want to share with as many people as possible.

To that end, in the next chapter I hand the book over to Theron so he can drive for a while. In it, he shares his personal thoughts directly with themed entertainment design professionals, including experience designers and students. But I believe *everyone* will want to read it because that's what we're doing here, as you know. Giving each side insight into the other, creating a broader and deeper view of what goes into a Disney experience.

Questions

1. What's one thing you can do at work to start incorporating what you've learned about how Disney does that?

2. What additional types of things would you need to do at work to make someone there say, "How does (insert your name) do that?"

3. What's one thing you can do at home to start incorporating what you've learned about how Disney does that?

4. What additional types of things would you need to do at home to make someone there say, "How does (insert your name) do that?"

5. When was the last time you really noticed a sunrise?

9

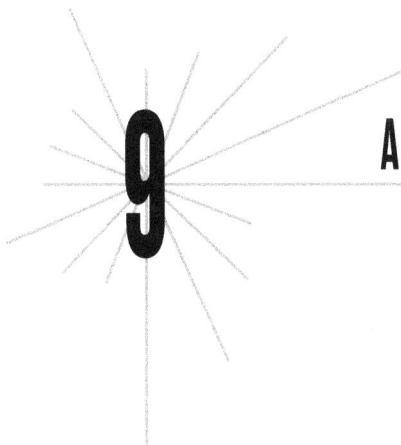

The Journey:
A Designer's Advice

"I think all artists——whether they paint, write, sing, or play music, write for the theater or movies, make poetry or sculpture——all of these are first of all pleasure-givers. People who like to bring delight to other people, and hereby gain pleasure and satisfaction for themselves."

Walt Disney

D iscovering what you want to do with your life is a journey and can mean different things to different people. Sometimes you find it by following in the footsteps of someone who has made an impact on your life and whom you respect. While other times, as is often said, the thing you do with your life finds you…and such was the case with my journey. At the time, though, I didn't realize what a huge impact a giant universe filled with worlds and creatures, battles in space between futuristic ships, and a tall scary guy with a breathing problem would have on my life and career.

It was 1977 and I couldn't wait to go to the movies and see a new space epic: *Star Wars*! I was 10 years old, sitting with my family eating popcorn, completely unprepared for how what I was about to experience would grab hold of my life so completely. To say I was blown away would be an understatement; I was transformed. That was the moment I realized I wanted to be a part of taking audiences into new worlds, telling stories, and creating experiences that transformed them as well.

Next, I threw myself into building models, honing my artistic skills, and reading everything I could find on filmmaking. I didn't want to star in films, I wanted to make them! One of my most prized possessions was the *Industrial Light & Magic: The Art of Special Effects* book by Thomas G. Smith that I got for Christmas. I read that cover to cover many, many times and, like throwing gasoline on a bonfire, my passion continued to gain momentum.

In my twenties, I landed roles thematically painting and sculpting sets on several films and television series. After a few years I discovered that, as a creative medium of expression, film itself wasn't giving me what I was originally passionate about. So when an opportunity came along to build new multi-dimensional worlds at Universal Studios Orlando as it was being built, I jumped there in 1990 and worked on projects like the central lagoon rockwork and the *E.T. Adventure* attraction.

As it turns out, taking leaps of faith like that into roles or even industries that I had no experience in became a hallmark of my career. And in that same spirit, in 1991 I joined Walt Disney Imagineering in Paris (named Euro Disneyland Imagineering) where I worked on their *Pirates of the Caribbean* attraction as a field art director.

On these different projects at Universal and Disney, I worked in a specialized area of creative fabrication called artificial rockwork. I don't mean to break any illusions, but all those mountains and walls of rock you enjoy in themed environments are...ahem, not real. They're designed and built by teams of extremely talented artisans and trades people.

That first role in Paris led to a 23-year career with Walt Disney Imagineering (WDI)...hard to believe looking back to when I was first hired, that I had never even heard of "Imagineering" before. I know, I'll give you a minute to process your shock...

Interestingly, every position I ever had with WDI for all those years, I had never done before. Art direction, production design, creative direction, executive leadership...all were new responsibilities. I also didn't have experience in attraction design; resort development; retail, dining, and entertainment (RDE); hotels; or nautical design (ships) before I took on those roles.

I'm emphasizing this point because I think it's important to be curious, to explore, and to try new things and to do it without fear. Never underestimate the power of your dream or the passion it takes to make it a reality. In fact, that's the first point I'd like to leave with you, which gets at the larger message I want to share.

That is, I'm writing this chapter because I want to inspire and inform themed entertainment design professionals, students, and even those who are currently working somewhere else in another role but want to take that leap into something completely new.

That "leap into new things" philosophy I preach was really put to the test, though, in 2020 when the pandemic hit and my career with Disney ended, as it did for many at that time. At that point, I launched my own boutique design consulting firm, and it has been one of the most rewarding moves of my professional life!

I founded The Designer's Creative Studio and have been working with clients from all over the world on a wide variety of projects, including re-imagining corporate branding; developing city-sized, immersive giga projects; teaching corporate executives how to build audiences instead of "customers"; and innovating ways to design narrative experiences. As I always say, in this industry one of your superpowers is that you must be adaptable. Every client is different. Every project is different. So, you must be flexible to succeed.

In my conversations with James over the last few years, we both realized how important it was to connect industry professionals with the fans they create the experiences for. After 30+ years in this amazing industry, I have witnessed time and again that nobody does it like Disney...and it's that experience that I'd like to share with you. My hope is to pass on some of the foundations and principles I learned there, to remind us all of what a privilege it is to be able to create experiences that bring joy to so many.

For those currently working in the industry

You realized your dream and have been building worlds, telling stories, and bringing escapism and play to generations. Your job has *real* meaning. Your contribution quite possibly affects millions of guests a year...but I bet you didn't think it would be so hard!

Going from one pressure-filled project to the next with never enough budget, people, or days in the calendar. Painfully cutting parts of the creation that you and your team really loved and that you just knew guests would love, too. Years in concept and design. Years in construction, including weeks sleeping under your desk, in your car, or on a stack of plywood during installation, testing, adjusting, and training.

Of course, staying inspired, curious, and filled with new ideas during all of this can be challenging. So I'd like to offer a few points of encouragement that kept me going—that kept the magic alive over the years and the miles and helped me encourage other team members to do the same.

Remember that our main job is to create experiences. At Imagineering, we were always very aware that, though it looked like Disney was selling stays at resorts, days at their parks, cruise vacations, movies, and songs, what Disney was actually selling were *experiences.*

Likewise, as subject matter experts in the themed entertainment industry (creative directors, project managers, set designers, architects, show managers, and so on), it's important that we remember that our focus is also creating these experiences. We all share a part in this process where we "dimensionalize" stories to create immersive, transformational experiences. And, at Disney, these physical, story-driven worlds connect audiences to the Disney brand in ways that build lasting memories and make guests excited to return.

Build an emotional connection. Because our work in the industry is complex and dynamic, it's easy to get focused on the processes, deadlines, and individual elements, and lose focus on building those memories. Therefore, I wanted to remind you that those attractions, restaurants, retail shops, and parades are far more than the sum of their parts. They represent a delicate balance of elements that are all different, but need to work together seamlessly, like an orchestra, to support the story narrative and make that connection.

Starting the project with this ideal of creating an emotional connection and keeping the team unified in this purpose throughout the project will make it much easier to be successful. It will also help ensure that we set our egos aside. Meaning that, as we design an experience, we focus on helping every fan feel immersed in the story, and not on growing our own name and fame or even the brand we're supporting (although, if we do our job well, all those things should naturally follow).

There are several primary reasons to create that emotional connection. First, when you tell stories that engage people's emotions, they naturally pay more attention to those stories. Next, these emotions, coupled with the sensory information we build into these experiences, will better lock that story into place in the guest's brain as a lasting memory. Then, future new experiences that bring up the same or similar emotions for the guest may bring up those memories, both strengthening—and building upon—them.

Bring creativity and business closer together. I firmly believe that creative teams need to adapt to see their practices more through a business filter, and business teams need to leverage a more creative-minded approach to their practices. This crossover will allow each to function at higher levels.

Taking this approach, creatives realize that no matter what type of project they take on, they will always be working for a client looking for their creative expertise to move the client's "business needle." For business teams, focusing on the creation of great experiences and building "audiences" instead of customers will help them reimagine their business and also give them the connection to their customer base that they truly want.

With all that, think how much easier projects would be and how much more value could be added if this overlap between creative and business happened more often.

Broaden your view. Developing our skills also gives us a much broader perspective. In my case, for example, working in the world of themed entertainment design, I have honed my skills through concepting, designing, and building theme parks, destination resorts, retail, dining and entertainment, and even cruise lines. Now, in my own company, I am incorporating these skills into an expertise I call Narrative Experience Design and using them more broadly for urban design projects, stadiums, future entertainment technology, and large-scale brand projects.

Start, continue, and end with story. As James and I mentioned earlier in the book, everything at Disney starts with story. And, as I see it, this is also a key principle for everyone in our field—to make story the backbone of everything we do, dictating all details of the experience and the environment it occurs in.

Now, would you believe that story itself—something people often consider to be non-technical, or "the soft and squishy creative stuff"—can drive profitability, brand equity, and customer acquisition? And that, really, it should be *the* mechanism that drives the whole project, becoming its "North Star" and ultimately the key to its business success.

As Imagineers, for example, we needed to get every element of the story applied in the environment just right to convince the guests that they were actually in the world we created. And this applied no matter how minor a detail might appear to be—whether it was the feeling of having dirt under their feet in a wilderness experience, sensing the low rumble of a spaceship in an outer space experience, or hearing the almost-imperceptible breathing sounds of the "animal" they're riding on in an other-worldly experience.

Everyone is a storyteller. At Disney, everyone in Imagineering is part of the storytelling process, from creative to finance to contract writing. Everyone. All 140 or so disciplines. That's because each role plays a part in delivering the story, as part of a larger group of highly specialized individuals with one goal—to connect guests to the experience emotionally and build memories that will last for generations.

Knowing how to tell stories is one thing; feeling empowered to share them with your colleagues or team members or even your family and community can be something different. Hopefully, you work with leaders and others who encourage your input and contribution.

I also recommend that you use storytelling to improve your daily communication with others, especially those that work in very different roles from you. As you do, remember that Walt named it "Imagineering" because it was a mash-up of "imagination" and "engineering"—two very different areas of expertise, but both needing to come together through storytelling!

The delight is in the details. We all know the saying, "The devil's in the details," but I like to believe that there's more delight in them. That's because when we as designers get those details just right, it gives the guest permission to let go of the real world and enter a fantasy, to "suspend" their disbelief and accept the fantasy as their current reality.

There are hundreds of thousands of details that must be considered when creating an experience, all of them orchestrated in a hierarchy so they feel completely natural. Of course, humans are very good at picking out details like these in an environment and deciding if everything is ok or not, and it's all processed constantly in milliseconds. So, our job is to make sure that the details of our constructed "story worlds" hold up to this level of scrutiny.

Now, I realize that not all companies invest in, or value, the same level of detail that Disney does. However, in those cases, I want to encourage you to still follow the process for developing these levels of story detail because I promise you that, over time, you will use this approach somewhere in the world for some client.

One of the first elements to apply this approach to in our work, for example, is the environmental placemaking and the time period. Are we in Africa? Or Antarctica? Or on an alien world? Are we in a city, village, or jungle? What types of trees would we find there? What language is spoken? What is eaten? How are the structures built? Out of rock? If so, what's the size and texture of the rocks? How do they fit together? Is it a village home made from wood? If so, are the walls and roof lashed together with vines? Are animal skins used for clothing? What kind of artwork would they have on the walls? Also, *when* is it? And on and on. Every detail matters.

Another benefit to considering all these details can be found if you're on a project that's over budget...If you've assigned hierarchical values to the details that were guided by the story narrative you've created, then you have a perfect road-map for mitigating costs while maintaining the experience.

Put the money in front of the guest. For professionals in this industry, focusing on emotional connection isn't just about memories. It's a design requirement.

For example, when I'm acting in the role of creative director, I focus on how the importance of building that emotional connection with fans translates into tangible requirements on the project, like always being aware of the budget. In fact, I can remember many times saying things like, "I don't want seventeen people to show up for the production meeting if we can do it with ten. I'd rather take the money we save and put it in front of the guests."

I did that because I wanted to put the most money from the project budget into elements that would be immediately recognized as part of the guest experience...by the guests themselves!

In a highly creative organization like Disney, and as a senior creative executive, I focused strongly on the money. Now, for some creatives, they might feel like that focus shouldn't be quite so strong if it takes away too much from creativity. But telling a leader in our industry not to focus too much on money is like telling a master chef not to focus too much on the temperature of their oven.

Why? Because money is just as important a component of any of our projects as the creative side. In fact, it's the tool that allows us to focus on those creative things. Not focusing enough on money may mean that, down the line, we may have to cut something important out. It would be like a chef going to all the trouble to pick out the right ingredients, make the sauce from scratch, and put everything together carefully, but forgetting that the oven isn't on or that it was set at too low a temperature.

While keeping the budget front and center, the project team, especially the creative side, needs to remember that the budget, like the schedule, is finite. I have worked with some creatives who thought the project budget was just a "guideline" and if they thought of a cool enough idea, the budget could be increased. See my comment earlier about creatives benefitting from more business acumen...

So, once the budget is set (assuming it's reasonable and aligned with the scope to be accomplished), all other aspects of the project can then be created with that budget in mind. That shouldn't make the team frustrated; it should drive them to be innovative, creative, and disruptive—thinking outside of norms and imagining solutions that take their client to new levels of success. Maintaining a positive, solution-oriented mindset will create scenarios of amazing breakthroughs and uncommon success.

To give an example of this solution-oriented mindset, there was this project where we had completed the design phase, it was out to bid with contractors, and then it was discovered we were over budget. It was then down to the creative team I led to explore options for reducing budget, mitigating costs, and finding the money without completely derailing the project or sacrificing all the hard work the team had done to create the perfect balance for the experience.

When, and if, you come to a point like this, the goal is for teams to not simply find a "quick fix" and say things like,

"Well, just remove all the trim," or "Let's use cheaper trees." Instead, if you've done your job well, you have a roadmap to go back to—one to help you decide what you can and can't do without. A way to be selective of what you keep, change, or remove, while still maintaining a strong experience for guests. Remember, the effort you take in solving a potential budget problem is as important as the effort you took to originally create the solution for the client.

By applying the principles I described earlier, having a clearly defined story direction as the mechanism for project delivery and creating a well-organized hierarchy of details, we were able to guide the project team to achieve the goal of reducing budget without sacrificing the experience. This accomplishment created a lot of team pride that I'm reminded of frequently whenever I revisit this venue.

Overall, it's true that the guest will never miss the ideas that don't get built in our projects. However, they *will* be able to tell if something is not created or executed well. Although this could be attributed to many factors, the highly experienced professional would not allow budget to be one of them.

That is why I believe this is the lens all industry professionals should look through—managing the project in such a way that the most money possible is put directly in front of the guests to create that emotional connection and keeping that as a guiding principle through all aspects of the project.

The guest plays an essential role in the story. This one can almost go without saying, but as James mentioned earlier in the book, in order to not take the things that can go without saying for granted, we sometimes need to say them! In this case, that means recognizing that, in any themed environment, the guest plays a critical role in bringing the story and that environment to life.

As Imagineers, yes, we created the foundation of the story, showing who lived there, the time period the story took place in, the primary action within the story, and so on. However, unlike books, movies, theater, or TV as storytelling mediums, the guests move through these themed environments as the hero of their own story!

To help them be that hero, we must provide all the elements they need to create their journey, but we can't make it so specific or pre-determined (like a movie) that they feel they can't participate. Or so open to their imagination (like a book) that they have to invent every element in their mind before their journey takes place.

And that's another reason why the worlds we create must be layered with so much detail and why it all needs the backbone of an amazing story—because any guest could be looking at any place at any time, focused on what matters most to them in that moment. The theme park environment itself then adds another level—as it comes to life in unexpected ways as many thousands of guests, all creating their own "story journeys," all at their own pace, visit the parks every day throughout the year all around the world.

This dynamic and ever-changing "performance" is part of the unique character of this industry. It also creates the memories that bring people back year after year, generation after generation.

For those who want to work in the industry

Because of the journey that led me to this industry, I look for opportunities to share my experience with students, young professionals, and those who want to transition into the industry from other roles, with the hope of supporting their journey.

When I do, I usually start with the question, "Do you really want to work in this industry?"

"After all," I tell them, "it's physically, mentally, and emotionally hard and can be unrewarding at times." I tell them this because, though they may have watched TV specials, read multiple books, and visited parks, dreaming about being in the industry, they may not have the perspective of the unvarnished reality.

So, my goal at that moment is to help them understand that, in this industry, you may work crazy hours and spend years and years on stressful projects with little to no break (except vacation time) between them. You may also feel like an idea vending machine, where you must have an ever-flowing stream of "concepts on demand" and often work for clients that may not fully appreciate your talent—or worse, believe they know better than you. So, again, "Do you *really* want to do this?"

I'm also testing their commitment at that moment, more for themselves, since I know from experience that anyone who answers "Yes" with a clear perspective of the challenges will be much more likely to be successful. After all, as in most if not all things, your "want to" is the key to how successful you'll be and, in this case, whether you'll be able to enter this industry and stay in it.

With that question asked and answered, I want to provide some tips about working in the industry that you might not learn in school or in your other roles. This includes lessons learned, highlighting challenges you may encounter and how to navigate them, and discussing ways to take advantage of opportunities when they present themselves and create opportunities when they don't.

Most importantly, I want to remind you that, as you move into the industry, your main responsibility will be to tell stories through designed and built worlds to create experiences— and that these experiences are meant to create memories and keep fans coming back. Also, remember that all of it is tied to business, too.

Now, before we go further, I think it's important to share more about my academic background because I have gotten a lot of questions about the different ways to enter and work in the world of themed entertainment design.

I spent two years in college and received a degree for that effort. However, I didn't continue with my education in a formal way because one of the best things I learned was that I flourish as a self-learner, pursuing the things I am most passionate about at my own direction.

But remember that my path isn't for everyone and every role. If you want to be an engineer or architect, you're going to need a license to practice and that takes years of formal education. I'm also not saying that an academic education isn't valuable; it definitely can be, *if* you choose that as your path. But the direction I chose was *my* path, and for some reading this, it might be theirs, too.

Be warned, though. Even with my approach, there are no shortcuts! The years of hard work with "formal studies" in a university are not avoided by taking the path I did—in fact, it might be even more difficult! The point I want to make here is that no matter what your approach is, we all need to be self-learners to be successful.

Indeed, a hard-earned degree may get you in the door, but the industry is so specialized and constantly changing, growing, and evolving that you will need to grow and learn constantly as well. In fact, that's a big reason why I always say that two of the most important "superpowers" you can possess, along with the adaptability we talked about before, are to be a great listener and to stay curious.

When you really listen to your client, for example, you can more easily discern what problems they want to solve and what their major business needs are. Then you can better process that information into the right creative solution.

Within your team, listening well, especially to those who are different from you, in role, in approach, in personality, etc., will cause the team's ideas and solutions to be better integrated at the group level. And the synergy of all these individuals coming together will ultimately make your team the best it can be—and ultimately can affect the success of your organization.

What does "not listening" on a project team look like? It might be where the creative people don't want to listen to the technicians talk about "capacitance" and "ohms" and the importance of cable shielding, and the technicians don't want to listen to the creative people talk about the "emotional connection of the story" or the importance of a "tone of pink" to the scene.

But what if they do take a minute to listen to each other? The creative person might adjust the tone of pink to fit with the technicality of the scene, and the technician might say, "Oh, I get it!" and understand why they need to adjust some things to better support the story. In that way, they hear past the specifics of the other person's role and listen instead to the heart and passion of what that person is communicating.

As for curiosity and the desire to learn, well, they both propelled me into some very interesting jobs where I made a living, but more importantly, I learned from many different experts in their fields.

Both curiosity and the desire to learn also definitely applied to the roles I held at Imagineering. With every new role I took on, it was something I had never done before...like art directing a whole theme park or leading the design of new ships. To direct the teams, partner with other leaders, and give solid guidance, I had to work even harder, do more research, find more people to learn from, and then get as much experience with the new skills as quickly as I could. All so that I'd be able to perform my new role in the best way possible.

Then, with every new role I had, I liked to say to my team, "Let's do the best work of our careers!" And once a project was completed, I would set the same goal on the next project and then the next role...chances were, it would be a completely different challenge.

Against this backdrop of listening, being curious, and

always learning, I wanted to share some things I wish I had known when I was starting out in this dynamic industry: the nuances, the possible speed bumps, and, most of all, the real secrets to navigating your career journey.

"Soft skills" are key. When applying for a job, we often focus mainly on the "hard" skills we possess, like using SketchUp, Photoshop, or Revit. In fact, many employers are guilty of focusing only on these skills, too, when they are interviewing and hiring. But I have repeatedly found, after interviewing and hiring countless people, that the skills we rely on the most as a team are the "soft skills."

Now, you might be saying, "Huh...what are those? There wasn't a class in my degree program labelled *Soft Skills 101.*" Well, these are the skills you will be required to use every day on a team to deliver those massive and complex, pressure-cooker projects. Working as a team player, you'll need to demonstrate such soft skills as commitment, delegation, listening, compromising, being willing to learn from others, admitting you don't know something, and more.

For myself, I know this is important because, looking back, there have been many people I chose to hire over other people who appeared to be more qualified on their resume. I did so because they had the right attitude, expressed a willingness to learn and adapt, and were passionate about being a part of our team. And, in the end, those were always the top performers. The ones who encouraged the team, helped others, and were relied on by everyone. Those were the ones who have gone far...and why I'm such a firm believer that the "soft" in "soft skills" is a misnomer.

Prioritize soft skills on your resume/curriculum vitae (CV). Knowing how important soft skills are, I always coach students to prioritize them over hard skills on their resumes. Why? Because many students going into the themed design industry will likely have similar hard skills. If those skills are important to the job you're applying for, along with whether you graduated from a top-tier school, then by all means highlight them. But know that the thing that will most often set you apart is your ability to demonstrate soft skills.

That's because, in my experience, soft skills are harder to recruit for and/or teach. They require a good amount of emotional intelligence and take time and focus to develop, which is why we look for people to come in with them to some degree. And that is also why I encourage students to capture, communicate, and beautifully represent their critical soft skills near the top of their resume—using that section to tell their story. After all, a resume is the "story of you."

When students do add that section, though, instead of just adding their soft skills in a bulleted list, I suggest they incorporate them into a small paragraph. That then creates a synopsis of who they are and why the employer should hire them. I also encourage students to weave those soft skills throughout the rest of their resume. It should catch the employer's attention, giving you a much better chance of getting noticed, getting interviewed, and getting hired.

Remember, a resume is the "knock on the door" of a company. Its purpose is to get you into the interview. That's when you can then knock their socks off by presenting the amazing "You"!

Show your process in your portfolio. Whatever your role, whether you're an artist, costume designer, architect, illustrator, or any other, make sure you have as much variety in your portfolio as possible. Show examples for as many styles as you can. And remember to highlight the process you used to develop some of those pieces. That will serve two purposes: to eliminate any concerns by the employer/interviewer about plagiarism, artificial intelligence-generated art, etc., and to specifically spotlight your background and thoughtful process.

This approach will also detail your part of a particular project and reinforce the soft skills you've described in your well-written resume. As much as a portfolio is about your work, if you're able to showcase how you contributed to a larger effort or how you collaborated with others to deliver something more than your part, it will exemplify how you would work on the potential employer's team.

Your first project is your most important project. It's been my experience that your first project at an organization is likely to be one of your most important ones there. It's the first time the leaders in the organization and your colleagues will get to see what you bring.

Also, as we just said about soft versus hard skills, your success on that first project and in your future career won't necessarily be based on what you produce. Yes, you'll need to demonstrate good, basic competency in your field and, yes, there will likely be latitude given to the fact that you're just starting your career. But there will still be a strong focus on how you develop relationships, deal with challenges, help others, provide updates and not surprises, and work with a variety of roles and departments. In other words, how you showcase the value you bring to the company. For example, if you're on the creative side, how well do you work with engineering and the client's maintenance team? And how do you act when times get tough? Are you a cheerleader or do you complain with others? Do you light lamps?

Be a lamplighter. In your new job, if times get hard for the team or organization, stand up and stand out. Be the person who can shake it off, refocus their vision, never let their light go out, and help others re-light their lamps. The one who doesn't believe in quitting, whose superpowers include adaptability, being willing to learn, listening, communicating, keeping the team motivated, and keeping the project's passion alive. If you can deliver those things, you'll be successful. And remember, you can't deliver something impossible like the "floating mountains of Pandora" without passion and playing well with others.

Again, as mentioned earlier, I can't tell you how many times I interviewed intern candidates and afterwards told my team we *had* to hire them, not because they were the most qualified in terms of hard skills, but because they not only demonstrated soft skills, but were "on fire"—meaning they were excited about the job, the projects they'd be working on, the team, really all of it. And I believed they could carry that fire to others in my group, especially during tough times.

Tension on a project isn't just probable, it's necessary. As long as there are different types of people and different types of roles on a project team, there will be tension. It goes with the territory. Especially when you look at the three main groups typically involved in a themed design project: creative, design, and delivery.

All three of these groups can have different visions, missions, implementation approaches, and requirements, and they may also be measured and rewarded differently. That can cause a lot of tension.

But that's ok. And to understand why, just remember the wisdom of Walt Disney when he chose his niche team of specialists from his film studio and named them Imagineers. They were creatives, technicians, engineers, writers, and more...a broad mix of the disciplines required to build the story-based, emotionally connecting worlds of Disneyland. And there was tension!

Of course, to succeed, the first step is to not allow that tension to become negative, or in other words, frustrate you to the point that it affects your work or way of working. So as much as possible, and as a team, keep the tension positive. Because positive tension drives us.

To know just how much it does, realize that any great company was originally built on positive tension; in Disney's case, Walt kept pushing the organization to accomplish more. Did they have some negative tension at the same time? Sure. You can't have a growing company or large, innovative projects and not have negative tension. But Walt, Roy, and their team worked constantly to ensure that, overall, they stayed on the positive side of the tension ledger.

Likewise, when I'm leading a team, I want there to be ongoing positive tension. As an example, think about any large, innovative themed design project and imagine how the conversation might go between those who come up with the concept, those who have to design it, and those who then have to deliver on that design.

You might hear someone from Design say, "We can't engineer something like that. The physics won't allow it." And the creative team might answer, "Well, ok, what if we did it in a slightly different way so it still gives that same overall experience, but with a more workable framework?" And then what if the delivery team added, "Yes, we might be able to do that, but just remember that we only have a $35 million dollar budget to work with, so, if we do what you're both discussing, we'll need to reduce the budget somewhere else."

That is how positive tension sounds on a project. Everyone working together, questioning each other respectfully, offering alternatives, and focusing on solutions, in a way that keeps the guest experience front-and-center—and may just win a few engineering awards along the way!

So, what does negative tension feel like? Well, I'm guessing that, even if you're early in your career, you've seen the effect of negative behaviors in a workplace, like not listening and communicating clearly, and being argumentative, and the effect that kind of tension can have not only on the work atmosphere, but also possibly on you and others both mentally and physically. To avoid this kind of tension, everyone has a responsibility to do their part and behave in positive ways, including those mentioned above. Remember, even if people don't have control over a certain part of the project or the entire work atmosphere, everyone still has a choice of how they show up.

Speak many languages. Yes, it's always helpful to actually speak different languages from around the world, especially when working on global teams. But what I really mean here is being able to speak at least the basics of "engineer" to the engineers on your team, "media design" to the media designers, "lighting design" to the lighting designers, "creative" to the creatives, and so on.

Because, if you really want to be understood, it's best to speak in the language of the person you're talking to, including the language of their field. It's also the best way to make a cross-functional team work.

At the same time, demonstrating this ability enhances your credibility and demonstrates your respect for different roles. Then, over time, if you're a good translator of a variety of these "languages," helping different areas talk to each other, helping clients understand how a project is progressing, helping suppliers and contractors know what's needed and why, and so on, then you'll be more effective, and you'll become even more valuable to your organization. It's also an invaluable skill to pack for your trip up the company ladder.

Mentors by any other name are just as valuable, if not more. Unlike others, I don't tell students they need to find a mentor in their new roles. That's because I, personally, have never gone out looking for official mentors in my own career. Instead, I worked to build relationships and organically learn from my leaders, the people on my team, and even people not associated directly with the particular project. The way I looked at it, everyone had something I could learn, therefore I could "curate" a type of mentorship from many different people.

For example, when I was an art director, someone on one of my project teams was an expert in show programming. Since I admitted I had little experience in that area, I asked if I could shadow her on the work she was doing. I also explained that, as I learned, it would allow me to give her more effective direction on a project we would be working on together. She happily agreed and I learned a ton!

In the end, then, admitting I didn't know something and seeking help from an expert who did provided the ability to successfully deliver the project and created a great working relationship. It also provided me with key skills I would use for the rest of my career.

And that's just one example. I try to always take that approach, being honest about the things I don't know and approaching people respectfully. And you know what? It works. They are typically open to it (we humans tend to be pleased when others value our knowledge and experience) and I've learned that everyone can teach me something that will make me better—and make me better for the team. I want you to have a similar experience because it has been so rewarding!

For those who taught me, I believe they also got something out of the relationship. For those working on one of my teams, for example, it typically encouraged them to take more risks because the boundaries between us were better defined. They also appeared to find an extra level of meaning in the project as experts teaching their leader. And, because of those two things, we formed a bond that wouldn't have formed in any other way. Then, looking at the benefits to the team overall, that approach tends to produce teammates who engage deeper in the story, are far more passionate, and who have relationships that stand the test of time. Of course, a strong, unified team can then ultimately create a much better experience for guests when the project is completed.

Another important benefit, though not the primary intent, can come when you use this approach. Namely, that your reputation can grow in your organization and across your field of expertise as you seek to learn from others, build your network, and acquire new skills and experience. To the point that, when an exciting project is about to launch and leadership is looking for someone for the team who has experience across multiple areas and has demonstrated the ability to build relationships, your name may just be more likely to come up...especially from those on the teams you've worked on because you took the time to leverage your soft skills, build relationships, and help others be successful.

Of course, I also have been open to, and looked for, opportunities to do the same for others. Have them shadow me on projects, sit with them to answer their questions, and so on. And after a long career, that approach has paid massive dividends professionally and personally, and contributed lots of meaning to my work. Who wouldn't want that?

Whether you're a professional or just starting out, remember two more things

First, remember that the best thing for the themed entertainment industry—and fans—is to keep a conversation going between both sides. The more we know about each other, the more we'll be able to create and enjoy experiences that build memories.

Second, remember that your job, whether you've already accepted it or will someday, is to give fans a "Happily Ever After." Actually, that's what Walt wanted for himself, for his daughters, and for all of us. To create a place where we could escape and play together.

In fact, as the industry originator, Walt's whole life prepared him for doing just that. From creating animated shorts to full-length animated movies. From live action to TV. Then through the medium of theme parks, which really were the full embodiment of the experience he wanted to create. And all along the way, he surrounded himself with amazingly talented people who, like him, believed in the power of creating experiences like Disneyland and, even after Walt was gone, the resorts all over the world, the Cruise Line, and more. He created a legacy where dreamers could dream and then make that dream real.

That's what I hope for you. That you'll find in this industry a way to turn dreams into reality—and back again—for fans and yourself.

What happens when you do? Well, for me, I think back to my childhood again. But this time, to Christmas. Our family was of limited means so, for Christmas, our parents would give us a choice. Get Christmas presents or go on a trip to Disney World.

We'd always pick Disney World.

Imagine *that*.

That is the industry you're either already in or will be entering.

P.S. I'd love to keep the conversation going as you either begin or continue your career in the themed entertainment industry.

LinkedIn: Connect with me at linkedin.com/in/theronskees.

YouTube: Watch my videos and subscribe at youtube.com/c/theronskees.

Website: Learn more about working in the themed entertainment design industry, check out my online course, and more, at design-erscreativestudio.com.

10

Touching the Hand That Touched Walt's

"In my business of motion pictures and television entertainment, many minds and skillful hands must collaborate...The work seeks to comprehend the spiritual and material needs and yearnings of gregarious humanity."

Walt Disney

When I started writing this book, I had an unspoken dream.

That one day I'd talk to someone who actually knew Walt.

But the dream seemed so far out of reach that I put it away, high up on the shelf near the other forgotten toys in Andy's room, like Wheezy and, sadly, for a time, Woody himself.

But two things helped bring that dream back down to within reach.

First, in completing the interviews for the book, I learned how interconnected many of the people in the Disney "universe" are. And second, I learned just how generous they were with their time, knowledge, and willingness to not only share their own stories but also connect me with others.

To the point that, with a nod to Kevin Bacon, I finally came within one degree of Walt.

He got on the elevator

Bob Berdin, a member of our *How Does Disney Do That?* group on Facebook, is a great example. He has supported our project for quite a while now, including generously giving of his time and introducing me to others. That includes connecting me with former Disney animator Willie Ito, who worked for Walt on such famous projects as *Lady and the Tramp*. And I probably don't have to tell you what it felt like to be sitting at home on the phone, vigorously typing, as Willie shared his story. Especially when he got to the part where, as a young man in search of his first professional animation job, he went to the Disney Studios and Walt got on the elevator with him.

When he shared that moment, I got goosebumps and whispered, "Wow," more to myself.

He then said, "Yes, that's exactly how I felt."

With that, here's Willie's story.

Willie Ito

"I was 19 years old when Walt Disney got on the elevator with me at Disney Studios. As you'd imagine, it was a pleasant surprise—especially because of what led up to that moment," recalls Willie Ito, former animator for Disney, Warner Bros. Cartoons, and Hanna-Barbera Productions.

"My Disney story really began when I was a kid, and I'd go to our local movie theater twice a week. For some reason, when a Walt Disney cartoon came on, I was enthralled. I think it was the way the stories were constructed and the characters were designed. You just fell in love with Disney cartoons! Whatever chance I had when Disney came out with a new film, I made a point of going to see it. When I did, I'd go alone because I knew I wanted to sit through it four or five times, eating popcorn and memorizing every little scene. I was mesmerized.

"Then I saw *Snow White and the Seven Dwarfs* for the first time—in living color! Especially the charm of Dopey and how beautifully he was animated. I knew right then, even as a kid, what I wanted to do with my life.

"And I stayed with that dream, even while being incarcerated with my family in internment camps for three years during World War II due to my Japanese heritage. In my years in the camp, there wasn't much to do behind those barbed wire fences, so I kept drawing.

"After we were released I took art classes through middle school, high school, and at the City College of San Francisco. At the college, my professor encouraged me to go into the animation business and wrote an introductory letter for me to the Chouinard Art Institute, a leading animation institution in Los Angeles.

"Around 1954 I went to Los Angeles and applied to Chouinard, which would later become part of the California Institute of the Arts (CalArts). Fortunately, I received a scholarship. My goal was to graduate in four years with a professional portfolio.

"Before I began classes, though, I took my student portfolio to the Walt Disney Studios in Burbank. I had always wanted to see the studio, so this was a great opportunity. And it was there, as I got on an elevator to have my first interview, that Walt got on with me. A pleasant surprise indeed!

"Afterwards, not thinking I'd get the job, I was ready to begin my studies and apply again in four years. But then I got a telegram from the studio two weeks later, asking me to come back and take an animation test. So I went back, passed, and was offered a job as an apprentice animation assistant on the 'Lady' unit, supporting Iwao Takamoto, who also worked on *Cinderella*, *Peter Pan*, *Sleeping Beauty*, and *One Hundred and One Dalmatians.*

"Of course I accepted, but I didn't know what the 'Lady' unit was, thinking it had to do with the ink and paint department that was staffed mainly by women. But I soon learned that it meant I'd be working on Disney's coming movie, *Lady and the Tramp*, and its spaghetti kissing scene in particular.

"Interestingly, at first the spaghetti scene wasn't going to be part of the movie. But Frank Thomas, a Disney animator, was so passionate about it being in the film that, at his own time and expense, he animated it himself. Then, when they ran the pencil tests, strung together in sequence, Frank had that scene thrown in. Walt came in unaware and saw that sequence and thought it really worked—so it stayed in!

"On that first assignment, I was an 'in-betweener,' meaning the animator would do the main drawings, like 3, 9, and 15. An assistant would put in more drawings between the animator's drawings. Then I would do drawings between the assistant's drawings. So for example, there may be a scene that has drawings 1, 3, 5, and 7 completed, and I would put in 2, 4, 6, and 8.

"Back then, of course, each frame was inked and painted. So the drawings had to be as perfect as possible so that they flowed seamlessly with the ones that came before and after. This was even more important because, when the drawings were then traced by an inker, there might be a small percentage loss in quality. That's very important to remember when you're working on a close-up of Lady eating spaghetti with her eyelashes fluttering, because that scene would then be blown up on the big screen many hundreds of times. Every flaw would be accentuated.

"I also remember at the time seeing other work in the studio going on around *Fantasia* and *20,000 Leagues Under the Sea*, and hearing about a new theme park that was being worked on—in secret—by the new WED Enterprises (former name of Walt Disney Imagineering).

"I then learned there would be a three-month lull between when *Lady and the Tramp* completed and work on *Sleeping Beauty* would begin, meaning I would be unemployed. So I called Warner Brothers. Because of my Disney portfolio and extensive training, they hired me right off the bat.

"After being there for a bit, my work was recognized by Chuck Jones, an eminent animator and director known for the *Looney Tunes* and *Merrie Melodies* series. He then picked me as an assistant animator for his unit, and I worked on many wonderful cartoons and characters like Bugs Bunny, Coyote and Roadrunner, and Marvin the Martian. After that I went into layout, started doing writing and directing, and also worked on *Beany and Cecil*, created by Bob Clampett.

"Then I joined Hanna-Barbera where I worked on *The Jetsons*, *The Yogi Bear Show*, *Josie and the Pussycats*, *Hong Kong Phooey*, *Scooby Doo*, *Huckleberry Hound*, the *Flintstones*, and more, before realizing I needed a break from animation.

"Later, after that break, I returned to Disney and joined their consumer products area as art director for the 800 Disney stores, eventually traveling to all of the Disney offices worldwide before returning for a bit to animation at the company.

"After I retired, I illustrated a children's book for a friend who was also interned in a camp during the war. He wrote about that experience in a wonderful book called *Hello Maggie* about a boy in one of the internment camps who adopts a baby magpie. The first printing of the book sold out, so we are now into the second printing. Plus, it's being made into an animated cartoon by Nemo Academy and Sheridan College in Toronto. Coincidentally, the animation supervisor also used to work for Disney. So here I am now, at age 89, overseeing production and merchandise as a producer on the animated film that is planned to come out in July 2024. Yes, I'm retired but busier than ever!

"Oh yes, I'll also soon be speaking at the Disneyana Fan Club meeting in California. Disneyana is a wonderful group made up of people who collect Disney merchandise and of former Disney artists, too. In fact, many of them know more about Disney than I do! At their last banquet, they graciously awarded me a Disneyana Legend Award.

"Looking back, I'd have to say that I always tried to take the bad and make it good. It started with how, during my family's incarceration, I chose to amuse myself by making cartoons. After all, we couldn't listen to the radio—it had been confiscated. We couldn't really listen to records. The only entertainment was that they would show current movies on Saturday nights in the recreation hall. Best of all, they always had a cartoon, like Disney or *Looney Tunes*, and that's what I lived for. Afterwards, I'd sit at our kitchen table in the camp and draw what I remembered from the cartoon.

"Fortunately, that desire never left me.

"And of course, that's why, from the time I was a young child, I felt such a warm place for Walt Disney Productions in my heart. Then, as I worked there, I could see that Walt Disney was a genius and could pick geniuses to work for him.

"In fact, of all the different people I've worked with in animation, Walt's staunch commitment to carefully constructed storytelling most stands out for me. In fact, I remember hearing one story from Roy Disney Jr. himself during my time at Disney that really illustrated Walt's commitment.

"As the story went, during the making of *Snow White and the Seven Dwarfs*, they were working on an elaborate sequence where the dwarfs built a bed for Snow White. At that point, in 1937, the sequence had cost about $250,000 to create. Walt sat through a screening of it and ordered that the sequence be removed.

"Walt's brother, Roy, who managed financing for the studio, apparently said something to the effect of 'Walt, that scene just cost us a quarter of a million dollars!' And Walt apparently replied that it had to come out because it didn't work and slowed down the pace of the film. So, out it came...

"That was Walt. For him, the story was the main thing. If anything detracted from the flow of that story, it would be cut. And I'm sure that throughout all his endeavors, like Disneyland, there were many very good ideas presented to him that didn't make it because Walt didn't think they really worked.

"And in my eyes, it's that commitment to story that brings a lump to our throats and a tear to our eyes when we go on Disney attractions and see Disney movies. Because Walt's original concept is coming through in that moment to the guests and audience. And it happens generation after generation.

"For me, it's definitely true, as I got a lump in my throat every time I took my kids, grandkids, and great grandkids to Disneyland—and saw them enjoying the rides.

"I was a small part of Disney, but I'm so proud of having been connected with a genius."

"There's a picture of my mom at Disneyland from 1955 that I love, especially because she was such a huge Disney fan," said Bob Berdin, long-time Disney fan and advisor to the board of the Disneyana Fan Club. "She is sitting with my two older brothers and my sister, dressed in her maternity smock because she was pregnant with me, on a bench on the drawbridge in front of Sleeping Beauty Castle. That's probably why I've always had an affinity for that area in the park, along with Snow White's Wishing Well. I was visiting the park even before I was born!

"I then went to Disneyland every year growing up. And my dad loved Disney just like my mom. In fact, he really admired Walt for his creativity. Later, as my wife, Rose, and I were parents ourselves, I became involved with the Disneyana Fan Club. At one of their conventions, as I had lunch with my son and daughter, an older gentleman sat down near us and started talking. He then started drawing Chip 'n' Dale on paper plates, explaining to my kids how to tell them apart. I later learned he was Disney Legend Bill Justice!

"Along the way I also met Sam McKim, another Disney Legend, animator, and mapmaker for WED Enterprises, and his sons, Brian, a Disney animator, and Matt, a former Imagineer, and daughter, Dorothy McKim, a Disney producer. I've also had the opportunity to meet Disney Legends such as Tony Baxter, Bob Gurr, Don Hahn, and Floyd Norman. Plus, I met former Disney animator Willie Ito at a Disney dinner and we've been friends since. In fact, I was pleased to be able to introduce James to Willie for the book.

"If you ask me why I love Disney so much, it starts with how I idolize Walt. There was just so much about him that was great. His talent. His innovation. Plus, I idolize Roy, too. They were a team. Meeting Roy Disney Jr. at a Disney Legends ceremony dinner was also a thrill.

"It's hard to put into words what Walt and the Disney company mean to me. I guess one of the best ways is to share a quick story. After the pandemic, the first place we went was Disneyland. While there, I went on the double-decker bus that drives down Main Street, U.S.A. Sitting in the front row on the top level, for just a moment, I felt like I was a kid again, riding the bus between my older brothers, like they were there with me. It's a magical place indeed."

Author's note: To learn more about the Disneyana Fan Club, go to disneyanafanclub.weebly.com. Based in California, the organization has chapters around the world.

He's been working on a railroad...Walt's

I briefly met Michael Broggie for the first time a little over a year ago at an event at Disney Springs hosted by The Carolwood Society. I had been invited by Jim VanOstenbridge, a board member of the society and member of our *How Does*

Disney Do That? Facebook and LinkedIn groups, who you heard from earlier in the book and who also has generously supported the project. The event featured former Imagineer Kevin Rafferty, author of *Magic Journey: My Fantastical Walt Disney Imagineering Career*, who held creative leadership roles on Cars Land, *Toy Story Midway Mania!, The Twilight Zone Tower of Terror, Mickey & Minnie's Runaway Railway*, and more.

Little did I know, though, that about a year later both Theron and I would be presenting our first *How Does Disney Do That?* workshop at EPCOT for an event produced by Jim and sponsored by The Carolwood Society. And that right before we presented, I'd sit down to interview Michael Broggie, author, co-founder of The Carolwood Society, Disney historian, and son of Walt's first Imagineer, Roger Broggie.

Or that, as I interviewed him, my wife and my son, Matthew, would be there, too. And to say that the three of us had goosebumps many times throughout that interview would not be an overstatement—especially as Michael shared his personal memories of walking into Walt's office as a child, and, along with his older brother, helping their dad as they worked with Walt on his miniature Carolwood Pacific Railroad at his house in Los Angeles.

But then, at the end of the interview, Michael gave me an unexpected gift, one that didn't cost anything but meant the world to me. I'll share more on that after we hear his story below.

Michael Broggie

"When I think about an early Disney recollection, I remember being about five and going to an employee Christmas party at the Disney Studios in Burbank, California," said Michael Broggie, Disney historian; author of *Walt Disney's Railroad Story: The Small-Scale Fascination That Led to a Full-Scale Kingdom*; co-founder of The Carolwood Society with his wife, Sharon; and son of the late Roger Broggie, a Disney Legend Award recipient who was selected personally by Walt Disney to be his first Imagineer.

"During the party, we'd typically see an animated film and short in their theater. This particular time, after the show, I remember walking out into the lobby and seeing Walt and Roy handing each child a wrapped Christmas box.

"When we got home, after taking off the paper, I found it was filled with Disney merchandise of that time, including whatever films or other promotions the company was doing. Being a kid, I got right into that box and played with everything. When it would break or wear out, I'd throw it away. Of course, now I wished we had locked it away as future 'Disneyana'!

"At the age of eight, my more direct exposure to Walt came in the backyard of his home on Carolwood Drive in the Holmby Hills suburb of Los Angeles. My father, Roger, and older brother, Roger Jr., and I were Walt's crew for his one-eighth-scale live steam miniature railroad, the Carolwood Pacific Railroad (as he called it), that encircled his home.

"The railroad started when Walt came to see my father in the precision machine shop at the Disney Studios. Whenever Walt would come in and ask him to do something, my dad would say, 'Oh, sure, Walt, we can do that.' In fact, that's why the title on the window honoring my dad on Main Street, U.S.A., in Disneyland starts with 'Can Do Machine Works...' Of course, then, after Walt left, my dad would have to figure out how to actually make it happen!

"To begin building the railroad, my dad turned to the company's master draftsman Eddie Sargent, a miniature railroader, and animators Ward Kimball and Ollie Johnston, who both had their own personal backyard railroads.

"Once Eddie drew up the layout, my dad took it to Walt, who laid the plans out on his dining room table. At that point, as I was told, with his daughters looking on, his wife, Lillian, began tracing the path of the track with her finger. When she came to one point, she stopped and apparently said, 'Wait a minute!' That's because she saw that the railroad would be going right through her rose and flower gardens, which were to be planted right outside the room Lillian had specially designed for canasta parties. Which is when she then said, 'No way!'

"Which was when Walt likely knew that he had a challenge on his hands. So he went back to his studio, called up someone in the legal department, and told him he needed a 'Right-of-Way' agreement—for his own backyard!

"Well, the legal fellow advised Walt that he didn't need an agreement since it was in his own backyard and California was an equal property state. To that, Walt said something to the effect that the lawyer didn't know his wife, and that he would still need the agreement. Lillian signed the agreement, and their daughters witnessed it.

"Even with the agreement, though, Walt still wanted to figure out how to have the railroad avoid the gardens, so he talked to his team. Jack Rorex, who was head of Studio construction, suggested building an elevated trestle in that spot or putting up a vine trellis, but neither would work because they would still affect the view of the gardens. So instead, they built a tunnel that was nine feet deep, five feet wide, and ninety feet long!

"Of course, Walt being Walt, he wanted his railroad to have story elements, including anticipation and surprise. So when they started constructing the tunnel, instead of going straight through, he had them engineer an 'S' curve into it. That way, when you entered the tunnel, it would be totally pitch black, since light wouldn't come through from the other end.

"What effect would that have?

"Well, I can tell you...because I remember personally riding into that tunnel as a kid, straddling a box car as it vibrated and waddled back and forth underneath me, hearing the engine chuffing and echoing off the walls of reinforced concrete block and plaster coating, and smelling the coal smoke—all while in total blackness.

"Then, as we went around that last curve, I could see a thin crescent of light up ahead—which started to grow until it opened into full sunlight. And right at that instance, I found myself on a 46-foot-long trestle, nine feet off the ground, looking down into a 150-foot canyon, rocking back and forth on this boxcar with no safety belt or hardhat!

"The finishing touch? Walt had made sure the telephone poles that were originally there were moved so they wouldn't spoil the view.

"Looking back now, of course, I realize how, with that railroad, Walt created an engrossing experience that touched all my sense impressions.

"As my family continued to 'crew' on Walt's train, I also remember how my brother and I had our own tasks. Like filling a bucket full of coal (shipped to Walt's house from Scranton, Pennsylvania, and ground down to 1/8-inch sized nuggets) and pouring it into the tender—at which point we'd also add water.

"After that, my brother and I would go up to the tunnel, where the railroad's freight cars were stored, ride them down into the 'Yensid Valley,' and then push them up the track to the steam-up table in front of Walt's red barn.

"I also remember how *anyone* could come to Walt's house and ride the train. Some days, there'd be 100 to 150 people there, and Walt wouldn't know one of them! But still they could ride. Of course, at that time, Walt hadn't yet become a national celebrity, which really happened when he started hosting his television show, *Disneyland*, in October 1954 on the ABC Network.

"For me, though, he was just my dad's boss. But I also remember calling him 'Uncle Walt,' something he insisted upon and liked. In fact, I felt like both my brother and I became like Walt's surrogate boys. Of course, he and Lillian had two daughters, Diane and Sharon.

"There are many things that made Walt great in my eyes.

"One was his genius for having an innate understanding of human nature. He knew what moved him. So, using his own judgment of what he felt an emotional connection to, he believed that other people would feel that same experience.

"For an example of how he understood human nature, as I heard the story, in one meeting at the studio Walt pulled out a cigarette and asked if anyone had a light. One of the new guys had a Zippo lighter, so he reached over and fired it up, and when he did the flame burned off half of Walt's mustache!

"Walt exclaimed, 'Are you trying to kill me?!' Then he went to the nurse to have the burn treated and have the rest of his mustache shaved off.

"Well, the young guy spent the whole rest of the day thinking he was about to get fired and should pack up his desk to be ready to leave. All the other guys were avoiding him. So the next day, as he sat in his office, when the phone rang and it turned out to be Walt, he thought his time was up. But instead, Walt asked him to meet him in the studio's commissary. And there, they had lunch together in full view of the whole staff.

"Walt did that because he wanted to send the message to everyone that everything was fine, and that people should associate with the young man. A great example of how Walt could solve an issue with one simple gesture.

"Two other things that made him great were his unbounded curiosity, how he took in everything, and how he treated children at an equal level. For example, I remember going into his office on the studio lot as a kid, where he had a five-room suite in the animation building. I'd ask Delores, his secretary, if Walt was busy. If he wasn't, I'd hear Walt's voice say, 'Send him in!'

"I'd sit in a chair in his office, where the shelves were filled with awards and citations from all around the world, including over thirty Academy Awards! As I sat there, Walt would ask me questions like what are you watching on television, what are you reading, and what do you like about different things? And it seemed like he would absorb it all. Which points to another thing that made him great—his photographic recall.

"For example, Ward Kimball would say that if you were in a meeting with Walt, and you retold something but changed the story, Walt would stop you and say, 'This is what you said before.' And he'd be right!

"In fact, he was noted for his incredible memory, including having accumulated his childhood experiences and having a total recall of what he liked and didn't. It gave him a guide to what the public found appealing, and he applied it in everything he did.

"He was also very good at finding solutions. For example, in the Story Department, they'd get to a part of a story but not know how to get beyond a certain point. So they'd call Walt in, and he'd review the storyboard and quickly figure out where it should go next, suggesting a twist here, a movement there. He had an amazing ability to cut right through everything and get to the solution.

"Another great thing about him: he listened and often acted upon what he heard. Which is one of his traits I have a personal memory of. It happened a few days after his studio Christmas party when I was eight. That year, at the party, instead of showing a feature film and cartoon, they had tumblers, magicians, and other live acts, then showed an animated short, *The Night Before Christmas.*

"Well, my father, brother, and I were at his house that next weekend, helping on the train. While I was standing in front of his barn, Walt came out, holding the yellow caboose he had personally built. He also had perfectly detailed the interior.

"Since I always enjoyed the films at the Christmas parties so much, when Walt set his caboose on the rails, I took the opportunity to tell him that I really hadn't cared much for the new show, explaining that I liked it better when films were shown.

"He looked at me and one of his eyebrows went up while the other went down (a gesture the people who worked for him knew well), almost like he was looking through me. Then he said, 'Well, you just can't please everybody,' and walked away.

"Back at home, I told my mother about the conversation. She was, of course, horrified that I had the audacity to criticize the Christmas party that was given for employees' children. So, she made me sit down and write out an apology letter to Walt, which my dad delivered to his office the next day.

"I never heard anything back, but guess what? The format of the Christmas party was back to films the following year! Proving that Walt had listened to his most audacious juvenile critic."

"The first memory I have of being in the same place as Michael Broggie was at the 2004 Walt Disney Company Annual Meeting in Philadelphia," said Jim VanOstenbridge, board member for The Carolwood Society, photographer, and solution architect.

"Eleven years later, I met Michael in-person for the first time at The Carolwood Society's booth at the 2015 D23 Expo. Just a year after that, thanks to the encouragement of now-retired Walt Disney World railroad engineer Joe Bopp, I started getting to know Michael and his wonderful wife, Sharon, at the 2016 Carolwood Society UnMeeting, which Joe produced that year.

"In the years since, I have served as an event producer for The Carolwood Society and have had the great privilege of getting to know Michael as a friend."

From the 2016 *Carolwood Chronicle* newsletter of The Carolwood Society: "Why an 'UnMeeting?' As Sharon and Michael [Broggie] would say, 'We've all attended enough boring meetings in our careers.' So, they created the annual UnMeeting. Gathering in the 'Carolwood Room' at the Wilderness Lodge, this is a time to get together, talk, have munchies, and whatever fun things happen to come up."

As I ended my interview with Michael and thanked him, he held out his right hand, pointed to it with his left, and said, "Here, shake my hand."

So of course, I did.

As we shook, he said, "There, now you can say you've touched the hand that touched Walt's."

After that, I just sat for a minute, quiet and grateful. Like a circle had been completed.

As the dream I had of talking with someone who knew Walt had come true.

Twice.

And somehow, I knew I'd never wash my hand again (ok, well, not really, but I sure felt like that. Maybe just Disney hand sanitizer from now on).

That moment also gave me the idea of how to finish the book.

With a letter to Walt.

Questions

1. Who is the one living person related to Disney you'd most like to meet?

2. What would you tell or ask them?

3. Who is the one person no longer living related to Disney (not Walt), you'd most like to meet?

4. What would you tell or ask them?

5. What would you most like to ask Walt and what would you most like him to ask you?

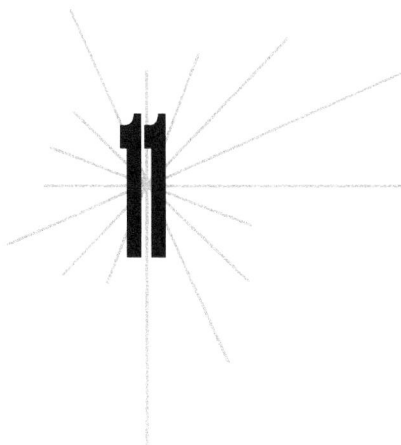

11

Dear Walt,

"...from time to time, I'd sense your presence, standing slightly behind me in that same office, just over my right shoulder...Then, I'd simply hear your firm, but encouraging, 'That'll do. Now, keep going.'"

James to Walt

D ear Walt,

Well, here we are, almost three years to the date since I first rode *Flight of Passage* and then asked myself, "How does Disney do that?"

What a long, amazing journey it's been since that day, filled with kind people, remarkable stories, starts and stops that seemed like the end of the road at times, and a thousand coincidences, big and small, thrown in along the way.

Of course, I'd be lying if I didn't admit that it's been hard at times. In fact, there were some moments when I felt like giving up, when I couldn't quite figure out what to do next, how to overcome a bump in the road that seemed more like an insurmountable barrier, or what this would all look like when it was done. Not just the book, but also the online groups, the website and workshops, all of it.

And it was in those moments where I'd most think of you, Walt. Of how much you went through in your own life as you worked to create something new—actually many somethings. And I knew, as one human knows about the other, that there were likely some pretty tough times for you in all of that—when you had to keep moving despite doubts from within and without, knowing that it's all too easy to lose faith.

Yes, it was in those moments that you truly became my mentor. I'd look to the left in my home office to a picture on the wall, a gift from my wife. You're in it, walking, smiling, hands in pockets as you "check out" the Florida construction site that would soon become the Magic Kingdom—with the future Cinderella Castle superimposed, and of course super imposing, standing behind you. Below it all, the word "Vision." And under that, your quote: "It's kind of fun to do the impossible."

True, it can definitely be fun to do the impossible. But at times, it can also feel, well, just impossible. To the point that, in those moments of doubt, I didn't know if I had it in me to complete the book. But *you* seemed to know.

At least that's what I felt when, from time to time, I'd sense your presence, standing slightly behind me in that same office, just over my right shoulder. You'd look at the words I had typed and the many that I hadn't yet (for a writer, facing the blank page is sometimes like walking into Mordor), assessing my work and its conviction as I imagined you doing with your animators. Then, I'd simply hear your firm, but encouraging, "That'll do. Now, keep going."

Yep, that was it. No long speeches. Nothing we'd probably find in a Walt Disney quote book. But still, when I needed it most, you were there.

You were there through my partner, Theron Skees, too. When we talked, he'd share his stories, and he'd do it passionately. To the point that I'd often tell him that listening to him was like what I imagined it must have been like to listen to you.

Now, Theron's a humble man, so of course he wouldn't accept that comparison. But still, I felt it.

And you were there through my wife, Gina. When we guested on the *Monorail Tales* podcast, for example, the first time we did so together for this project, the co-host asked us both what our favorite Disney characters were. I said "Donald Duck" because I just like his cantankerous attitude. After pausing thoughtfully, Gina answered, "Mickey Mouse," because as she put it, "Mickey is Walt to her." I had never heard her say that and it seemed to come both through her and from somewhere else, too. A message of sorts. And something about the earnestness of her answer marked that moment for me, as if, once again, you were there, too.

So, for being there, standing over my shoulder and helping me stand on the shoulders of others, I thank you.

Oh, yes, and thank you...

...for what you did for all of us everywhere. When you sat on that bench in Griffith Park, thinking about a place where families could have fun together. As you know if you've been reading this book (and since you're my virtual mentor, I know you have), at that moment with your daughters, I'm pretty confident you weren't considering how much money such an endeavor would bring. No, I believe you simply wanted us to feel what you were feeling.

...for being that man sitting on that particular bench who had once been a child walking a paper route deep in the early morning and after-school Kansas City snowdrifts, hauling newspapers on a sled, knowing he wouldn't even be allowed to keep the money he earned. As he trudged forward, playing with toys he'd sometimes find on people's porches because he had few, if any, toys himself—or even the time to play. And for transforming those difficult moments for him into moments of belonging and joy for all of us. Ultimately, giving my family and so many others a place to grow close and call our "second home."

...for inspiring me personally by being a father who adored his daughters, giving them the most important gifts a parent can offer their child: time and attention.

...for helping me remember. Because, as I reflect back on that day on *Flight of Passage*, I realize that it was also my "rite of passage," just in reverse. Not a child becoming a man. But a man becoming a child.

Ok, I know that's a lot of "thank you's," Walt, and that it's getting late, but I've got just two more.

You see, when I ended my interview with Michael Broggie, he shook my hand and said, "There, now you can say you've touched the hand that touched Walt's." I was stunned, because it literally felt like some final tumbler had fallen into place. One that started with my question to myself, "How does Disney do that?"

And though in this book we've heard many answers to that question, I do believe, as mentioned before, all of them eventually circle back to one.

"With love."

The same love I believe that...

...you felt and wanted to share as you watched your daughters on that carousel.

...your Disney Studios team felt and still feel as they brought and continue to bring your stories to life with pen, ink, paint, multiplane camera, computers, and more—literally giving breath to every character, song, sidekick, and scene.

...your Cast Members demonstrated and continue to demonstrate as they do anything surprising and kind for a guest, like returning a daughter's purse when most any other place on the planet would just offer a coupon for free tater tots at the snack bar.

...your Imagineers revealed and still reveal as they created and continue to create experiences to help us feel all things under the sun, and many things above it, like wonder.

So, for all that, Walt, thank you.

Oh, and please thank your brother, Roy, for me, too. A big brother who, throughout his life, demonstrated one thing over and over again. That though it seems to have started with a mouse, or in my case a banshee, it really started because two brothers simply loved each other.

Take care,
James

See Ya Real Soon!

Stay connected through our online groups

As mentioned way back in the Introduction, though you're at the end of the book, you're really at the beginning...of a conversation. One you can take part in by joining our online groups on Facebook and LinkedIn (which, because it's on a professional platform, focuses more on the brand aspects of Disney but, at its core, is still about emotional connection) and by following our Instagram page.

I'm personally posting and interacting in the groups almost every day, as are many of the contributors you've seen throughout the book. We'd love to have you join us. When you do, please let us know that you've read the book!

Facebook: facebook.com/groups/howdoesdisneydothat

LinkedIn: linkedin.com/groups/12646123/

> *(Yes, I wish LinkedIn had personalized URLs, though "12646123" does have a certain Disney "ring" to it)*

Instagram: @howdoesdisneydothat

Share your story for future books in the series

Many of the stories in this book came from members of our online groups and website. So, I'll be continuing to gather stories for future books in the *How Does Disney Do That?* series.

In fact, we're already at work on the next one, which will focus on Disney Cast Members. So, if you have a story of how a Disney Cast Member strengthened the emotional connection you have with Disney, you're a former Disney Cast Member who has helped create that emotional connection for guests, or you simply have a story that relates, please share it either through our groups above or directly to us at our website: www.howdoesdisneydothat.com. By the way, I don't include stories from current Disney employees, in order to be respectful of the company.

Additional topics in the *How Does Disney Do That?* series may include the following:

- Disney Cruise Line
- Disney International
- Disney Cuisine and Libations
- Disney Movies, Art, Songs
- Disney Merchandise
- Disney Live Entertainment
- Disney Special Programs (e.g., Adventures by Disney, Disney Vacation Club)

If you have stories related to any of the other topics above, please don't hold back—send them in through the groups or the website along with a note as to which topic you feel it belongs in, such as the Cruise Line.

Stay connected with Theron Skees

Themed entertainment design professionals, students, fans, and others can stay connected with Theron Skees through these channels:

LinkedIn: Connect with him at linkedin.com/in/theron-skees.

YouTube: Watch his videos and subscribe at youtube.com/c/theronskees.

Website: Learn more about working in the themed entertainment design industry and check out Theron's online course, and more, at designerscreativestudio.com.

Resources for Disney Fans, Themed Entertainment Design Professionals, and Students

Resources for Disney fans

I came across lots of great resources during the course of researching the book, so I wanted to share those with you. Any item with an "*" indicates that someone connected to that resource contributed a story to the book.

Books

Choose Your Own Autobiography by Neil Patrick Harris (Crown Archetype, 2014)

Disney's Land: Walt Disney and the Invention of the Amusement Park That Changed the World by Richard Snow (Scribner, 2019)*
 Learn more at richard-snow.com.

Drawn to Greatness: Disney's Animation Renaissance by Michael Lyons (Theme Park Press, 2022)*
 Learn more at wordsfromlyons.com.

Every Guest is a Hero: Disney's Theme Parks and the Magic of Mythic Storytelling by Adam Berger (BCA Press, 2013)*

Gift of Life by Henri Landwirth (Give Kids The World Village, 2009)

Hello Maggie! by Shigeru Yabu, illustrated by Willie Ito (Yabitoon Books, 2007)*

Hidden Mickeys: A Field Guide to Walt Disney World's Best Kept Secrets by Steve Barrett (UNKNO, 2015)*
 Learn more at hiddenmickeyguy.com.

How's the Culture in Your Kingdom?: Lessons from a Disney Leadership Journey by Dan Cockerell (Morgan James Publishing, 2020)*
 Learn more at dancockerell.com.

The Imagineering Pyramid: Using Disney Theme Park Design Principles to Develop and Promote Your Creative Ideas by Lou Prosperi (Theme Park Press, 2016)*

> Learn more at imagineeringtoolbox.wordpress.com.
>
> (*Author's note*: Thanks for introducing me to Rivershore Press, Lou!)

The Imagineering Story: The Official Biography of Walt Disney Imagineering by Leslie Iwerks (Disney Editions, 2022)

> The accompanying series and *Behind the Attraction* series is on Disney+.

The Making of Disney's Animal Kingdom Theme Park by Melody Malmberg (Hyperion, 1998)

The Official Walt Disney Quote Book by Walter E. Disney (Disney Editions, 2023)

> Many of my introductory chapter quotes came from this excellent book.

On Purpose: How Engagement Drives Success by Pamela Landwirth (Give Kids The World Village, 2019)*

> Learn more at pamelalandwirth.com.

They Drew as They Pleased by Didier Ghez (Chronicle Books, 2015)*

> Learn more at didierghez.com.

Walt Disney: An American Original by Bob Thomas (Disney Editions, 2023)

Walt Disney's Missouri: The Roots of a Creative Genius by Brian Burnes, Dan Viets, and Robert W. Butler (Kansas City Star Books, 2002)

> Dan Viets is president of "Thank You Walt Disney, Inc."*
>
> Learn more at thankyouwaltdisney.org.

Walt Disney's Railroad Story: The Small-Scale Fascination That Led to a Full-Scale Kingdom by Michael Broggie (Pentrex Media Group, 1997)*

> Learn more about Michael's other Disney-related books on Amazon or other online sites.

Walt Disney: The Triumph of the American Imagination by Neal Gabler (Vintage, 2024)

The Walt Disney World Trivia Book: Secrets, History & Fun Facts Behind the Magic (Volume 1) by Lou Mongello (UNKNO, 2004)*
> Learn more at loumongello.com and wdwradio.com.

Women of Walt Disney Imagineering: 12 Women Reflect on their Trailblazing Theme Park Careers, (Disney Editions, 2022)*

Podcasts

Creating Disney Magic
> jodymaberry.com
> Co-hosted by Lee Cockerell, former executive vice president of operations for Walt Disney World, and Jody Maberry, consultant, speaker, and business and podcast coach.*

Hangin' at the Hangar Bar
> facebook.com/Hanginatthehangarbar/
> Scott Minks, former Disney Cast Member, hosts the podcast.*

Imagination Skyway show and community
> imaginationskyway.com
> Matthew Krul, former Disney Cast Member, hosts the podcast and community.*

Mitlin Money Mindset
> mitlinfinancial.com/insights/blog/category/podcasts/
> Larry Sprung, wealth advisor and Adventures by Disney participant, hosts the podcast. Theron is featured on one episode.*

Monorail Tales
> monorailtales.com (Learn more about the podcast co-hosts at the site.)
> *Fun fact*: This was the first podcast my wife and I appeared on together for *How Does Disney Do That?*. It's also where she gave the answer that shows up in this book's "Dear Walt," section.

WDW Radio Podcast
> wdwradio.com.
> Lou Mongello, author, speaker, and consultant, hosts the podcast.

Sites, pages, and groups

The Carolwood Society website

From carolwoodsociety.org: "The Carolwood Society is dedicated to preserving the personal railroad legacy of Walt Disney."

Michael Broggie is co-founder and chairman and Jim VanOstenbridge is a board member and event producer.*

Disney Day Drinkers Club Facebook page

facebook.com/groups/disneydaydrinkersclub, owned by Skip Sher.*

Former Imagineer Brian Collins' website*

wdwwithme.com and brainstorm-institute.com

Get Down to Disness website

getdowntodisness.com (resources for travel agents who plan Disney and Universal vacations)

Kat Wolfe, founder*

Give Kids The World Village® website*

gktw.org

Join the *How Does Disney Do That?* fundraising campaign for GKTW at give.gktw.org/fundraiser/4894291.

A portion of the proceeds from this book are going to GKTW.

Master woodcarver of Disney signs (and more)

woodcarverguru.com

Ray Kinman is a professional woodcarver, teacher, and independent Disney artist.*

Orlando International Airport (MCO) Facebook page

facebook.com/flyMCO

Fun fact: Why is an airport's social page in this book? Because it's one of the best-run, funniest pages I've seen and, not surprisingly, it's often Disney-related.

Sparkcatcher blog and Facebook page

sparkcatcherblog.wordpress.com and facebook.com/sparkcatcherblog/

Written by former Disney Cast Member and Disney historian Nathan Eick.*

Theme ParkLife Facebook page
facebook.com/ThemeParkLifeFan/
Owned by Aydin Turgay.*

VanOMedia photography website*
vanomedia.com, includes wonderful Disney photography
Owned by Jim VanOstenbridge, board member of The Carolwood Society.
Also access Jim's site through howdoesdisneydothat.com/gallery.

Walt Disney Birthplace
thewaltdisneybirthplace.org

Walt Disney Family Museum
waltdisney.org

Walt Disney Hometown Museum
waltdisneymuseum.org
Christopher White, museum board member, is a former Disney Ambassador.*

Magazines, media, TV, and more

Magic Moments Monday articles on LinkedIn
Search "Doug Rabold" and "#magicmoments" on LinkedIn.*

Pioneers of Television series (including episodes with Tim Allen, Robin Williams, Dick Van Dyke, and more)
Learn more about this series and producer Steve Boettcher at pbs.org/wnet/pioneers-of-television/.*

WDW Magazine (Walt Disney World), *DLR Magazine* (Disneyland), and *DCL Magazine Blog* (Disney Cruise Line)
Learn more about the magazines, owned by Stephanie Shuster, CEO, and Danny Shuster, creative director, at wdw-magazine.com.*

Resources for themed entertainment design professionals and students

In this section, Theron Skees and I share helpful resources for themed entertainment design professionals, students, and others. Many were taken from Theron's courses, *How to Work in Themed Entertainment* and *Masterclass Series: Developing a Story for Show Business*. Learn more at designerscreativestudio.com.

Books recommended by Theron

The American Amusement Park Industry: A History of Technology and Thrills by Judith A. Adams (Twayne Publishing, 1991)

Creativity, Inc.: Overcoming the Unseen Forces that Stand in the Way of True Inspiration by Ed Catmull and Amy Wallace (Random House, 2014)

Designing Disney: Imagineering and the Art of the Show by John Hench with Peggy Van Pelt (Disney Editions, 2009)

Designing Disney's Theme Parks: The Architecture of Reassurance by Karal Ann Marling (Flammarion, 2001)

Dream It! Do It!: My Half-Century Creating Disney's Magic Kingdoms by Marty Sklar (Disney Editions, 2013)

Drive: The Surprising Truth About What Motivates Us by D.H. Pink (Canongate Books, 2018)

The Experience Economy: Work Is Theater & Every Business a Stage by B. Joseph Pine II and James H. Gilmore (Harvard Business School Press, 1999)

The Fantastical Engineer: A Thrill Seeker's Guide to Careers in Theme Park Engineering by Celeste Baine (Professional Publications, 2004)

Industrial Light & Magic: The Art of Special Effects by Thomas G. Smith (Del Ray, Ballantine Books, 1987)

Leaders Eat Last: Why Some Teams Pull Together and Others Don't by Simon Sinek (Penguin Business, 2019)

Learning from Las Vegas: The Forgotten Symbolism of Architectural Form by Robert Venturi, Steven Izenour, and Denise Scott Brown (MIT Press, 2006)

Made to Stick: Why Some Ideas Survive and Others Die by Chip Heath and Dan Heath (Random House, 2010)

One Little Spark!: Mickey's Ten Commandments and the Road to Imagineering by Marty Sklar (Disney Editions, 2015)

The Power of Myth by John Campbell, Bill Moyers, and editor Betty Sue Flowers (Turtleback Books, 2012)

Start with Why: How Great Leaders Inspire Everyone to Take Action by Simon Sinek (Portfolio Penguin, 2019)

Theme Park Design & the Art of Themed Entertainment by David Younger (Inklingwood Press, 2016)

Walt Disney Imagineering: A Behind the Dreams Look at Making MORE Magic Real by The Imagineers (Disney Editions, 2010)

Websites recommended by Theron

Funworld magazine

    funworldmagazine.net

    Magazine of the International Association of Amusement Parks and Attractions (IAAPA) at iaapa.org.

Themed Entertainment Association (TEA)

    teaconnect.org

InPark magazine

    inparkmagazine.com/category/themeparks

Imagineering in a Box

khanacademy.org/humanities/hass-storytelling/imagineering-in-a-box

According to Disney Parks Blog: "Imagineering in a Box is a free online program that brings together the diverse talents of Disney Imagineers around the world for a one-of-a-kind learning experience and is part of Disney's commitment to helping today's youth create the future they imagine."

Planet Attractions

planetattractions.com

Park World magazine

parkworld-online.com

Pixar in a Box

khanacademy.org/computing/pixar

According to pixar.com about this free online course: "Pixar and Khan Academy have collaborated to create, develop, and promote a series of learning tutorials that demonstrate how traditional school subjects such as math, science, and the arts are a vital part of the everyday work put into Pixar's filmmaking process."

Themed Attraction

themedattraction.com

Industry news, articles, and podcast featuring in-depth discussions with designers and other professionals.

And just a few more...

Former Imagineer Colette Piceau's website*

itaintshakespeare.com

Former Imagineer Josh Steadman's website*

steadmanstyles.com

Zeitgeist Design and Production

zeitgeist-usa.com

Ryan Harmon is president and chief creative officer, and Joe Lanzisero is executive vice president and chief art director.*

Contributors

Appreciations

From James

So, why *Appreciations*?

Well, as you know, most books have an *Acknowledgments* section. But, after Theron reminded our workshop audience at EPCOT to not only recognize—but appreciate—a sunrise, it dawned (pun gloriously intended) on me that I didn't want to just acknowledge the people who helped me on this book's three-year journey, but to *appreciate* them.

To start, therefore, let's go back to the beginning. To my wife, Gina. And, yes, I know that spouses and other significant others often come at the end of a section like this, but I was never a big fan of that approach. Because, really, who lives more with the day-to-day grind and griping of someone writing a book than the people closest to the writer?

For Gina. As I've said, she really introduced me to Disney when we first met, and it has been a big part of our relationship ever since, including buying a *Pinocchio* print, our first major purchase together, on the night we got engaged, dancing with everyone to "Kiss the Girl" at our wedding reception, taking regular Disney trips as the kids grew up, and her gently prodding me to watch all the Disney classic animated movies I had missed during my childhood. With this book, specifically, Gina helped me get at the heart of what I wanted to say without it sounding like a thesis paper, and often was my "focus group of one."

So, are Disney princesses real? Well, if that means someone

who could literally light up the Cave of Wonder with her smile, didn't mind when I stopped every twelve feet while walking through a Disney park or resort to make another note or take another picture, advised me on when *not* to send a second follow-up email because I was antsy, created amazing cocktails at strategic points along the way, and also made the "Monorail Dress" one of the most talked about topics when Theron and I presented at EPCOT, well, yes, I do believe they are. And Gina is.

For my children. Jeremy. Matthew. Alexandra. Three names that are really one for me, naturally flowing together. Not only do I appreciate them for being kind and courageous, but for everything they've contributed to the project, including giving me permission to share their stories and "look back" quotes, their "growing up at Disney" photos in our online groups, and more. I couldn't be prouder. Gina, of course, feels the same.

For our granddaughter, Penelope, who is allowing us to see Disney for the first time—once again.

For my family and friends, including my sister and brothers and their families, and my mother-in-law, who have been there for me in many different ways, participating in our online groups, providing encouragement, celebrating the moments. All of it.

For my mother and father, who are no longer here, but still are.

For Joe Rohde, who turned me back into a boy that day on *Flight of Passage*. He also graciously wrote the Foreword for this book, completing the circle.

For Theron Skees, my business, speaking, and writing partner. A few years back, during the first of our countless conversations, I gushed, saying that, as a Disney fan, I looked at Imagineers like rock stars. And, yes, I know many Imagineers are way too humble to agree to that categorization, as was Theron, but in my eyes, he actually is one. The themed entertainment design equivalent of Bruce Springsteen!

For my publisher, Barry Hill, at Rivershore Press, who also created this book's beautiful interior design. Thanks to Lou Prosperi, a fellow Disney-focused author, who introduced me to Barry. Sometimes the stars align and generous people appear. And Jonathan Hill, also at Rivershore. Yes, thank the Phoenicians for our A-B-Cs, but thank *Jon* for the wonderful cover design of this book.

For my agent, Joe Durepos, who I've known for over 20 years. To say he knows his stuff and has represented big authors on big books would be an understatement. He has spent hours with me patiently explaining everything from the scintillating details of book contracts to the exciting world of international rights. Just knowing he's got my "literary back" reassures me.

For Jim VanOstenbridge, who went from fellow fan to friend and also gave Theron and me our first opportunity to present together at EPCOT for The Carolwood Society. And Adam Berger, Brian Collins, Lawrence Ferguson, Michael Lyons, Scott Minks, and Dave Snell, who were all there from the beginning.

For Michael Broggie, who Jim introduced me to. Since

Michael shared his stories of "Uncle Walt" with me and shook my hand with "the hand that touched Walt's," the goosebumps still haven't gone down.

For Willie Ito, who went from World War II internment to riding an elevator with Walt, then working for him. And Bob Berdin, who introduced me to Willie. Bob is generous like the sky is blue.

For *all those* who shared their stories for this book. If you want an idea of their depth and breadth, check out the list of contributors on page 328. And like an exciting game of Disney Tag, almost every person I talked to referred me to someone else.

For everyone at Give Kids The World Village® who gave me stories, a tour, and a sense of wonder that somehow perfectly aligned with what I felt on *Flight of Passage*. If there's anything more important to all of us than fulfilling the wish of a critically ill child, I haven't found it yet.

For Abraham Maslow. I know there is already a pyramid on the *Seven Wonders of the World* list. But I do believe his deserves a runner-up award, at least.

For you. Because without a reader, a writer is just tossing words at the wind.

And, finally, of course, for Walt and Roy, and Disney itself.

From Theron

I'm glad James titled this section *Appreciations*, as it seems so appropriate after all the collaboration, talking, and dreaming we've done over the last few years together. In the same way, Imagineers, as creators, collaborate with, and are intrinsically dependent on, the guests and fans who enjoy their creations. So, you could say they truly *appreciate* one another.

In this spirit, I would like to express my gratitude and true appreciation for my Creator. I have gotten such joy and inspiration from Him and His creation and have been grateful for His guidance.

I also must recognize my wife, Judy, who has been there every hour, every day, through all the adventures, the tough and the tougher...the joyful moments and the sheer mountain-top experiences that were unparalleled. From moving a family of six to two foreign countries and learning how to do life there, to every business trip and every 70-hour week, when it felt like we never saw each other...to leaving corporate life and starting my own company. She's my best friend, my wonder woman, and I've been blessed to navigate this life with her for 36 years! It's her reassurance and encouragement that have propelled me.

For my four children, I appreciate every stage of our journey. They matured me in ways nothing else in life could and formed the best "sounding board" for every project I worked on at Disney! Their excited feedback from early story development through the finished product was invaluable. Even when my oldest daughter, a teenager terrified of *Tower of Terror*, joined our family on the ride during the Imagineering preview in Paris. To this day, that terrified teenager in the ride photo we took encourages me to move past my fears and discomforts to support something larger and more important, reinforcing a family saying, "People are more important than things."

For Disney. I'm so appreciative of the opportunity to have learned, practiced, and implemented with them at the highest level. To be given permission to take risks, explore and be curious, to lead amazing people, teams, and projects, and be given the responsibility to be trusted with so much. My 23 years with Imagineering formed how I see business, customer service, experience design, and the true needs of a client—to understand the end-to-end journey and create at the highest level. I learned to expect a lot from myself and the teams I led because the company expected a lot from me.

For my fellow Imagineers, although there are too many to name personally. Those who were friends, teachers, and mentors, and even those who were challenging. I appreciate learning something from them all. Now, when I say "Imagineering," you may immediately envision an environment of design, finance, planning professionals, and others. You'd be right, those team members held great influence. However, I'm also thinking about the folks who delivered the mail between our very spread-out offices, custodial teams that kept those spaces clean, and more. It's incredible how much I learned from them, too!

For the Disney guests and their endless hunger for new

experiences and opportunities to escape, play, and be genuinely blown away! Without this positive pressure to innovate, create, and constantly better myself, I would definitely be a different version of myself today. In large part, the guests are just as responsible for my growth, education, and refinement as my fellow Imagineers. In fact, I recall Marty Sklar sending me guest letters through the years, mainly containing questions and sometimes concerns. That's when I really learned that the guests thought of Disney as *their* land—their home away from home. Those letters taught me that guests not only deeply cared, but that I shared in the responsibility to deliver the Disney brand promise to each of them. Heavy!

For students and the next generation of theme park professionals. I have enjoyed teaching, lecturing, mentoring, and being a part of the journey for so many passionate people who pursue joining this industry. Their fresh outlook, inquisitive minds, and desire to learn helped me distill what I had learned through the years so that I could pass it on. It's so important to not only preserve what current and previous generations have created, but to allow these new professionals to stand on the lessons we've learned and then do even more. I can't think of a better way to leave a legacy than to impart the great joy I have experienced from my time as an Imagineer to others and to encourage them to do the same.

For James and his quest to understand the *how* and the *why* of Disney experiences that provide all of us with such precious memories. It's through the process of writing this book that we answered a lot of those questions for ourselves in the process! I am also grateful for the opportunity to "unpack" all of my knowledge and experience by focusing on the impact it has had on the guests...it has been a wonderful experience, James. Thank you.

Finally, I too am thankful for you, the reader. I hope you have enjoyed my contributions, but I also hope that you are taking away lessons you can apply to your professional and personal life. One of the biggest lessons I hope you take is how this book even got written in the first place. Two people from different backgrounds, living in different states at the beginning, with different professions, who met at the crossroads of "creating" and "experiencing" and both felt a transformation through this process. The common denominator was Disney, and our superpower was listening. I hope this encourages all of you to do the same!

About Us

James Warda, author of *Where Are We Going So Fast?: Finding the Sacred in Everyday Moments*, has written for the *Chicago Tribune, Chicken Soup for the Soul,* and Pioneer Press, and has contributed to numerous Disney publications and sites including *Celebrations* magazine, *Disney Magazine*, and *WDW Magazine*. He is a speaker and workshop facilitator, a former adjunct professor at Loyola University Chicago, and guest speaker for DePaul University of Chicago. A professional musician on the side, James has served in executive communication and marketing roles for several Fortune 100 companies, a national nonprofit, and a number of advisory boards.

Theron Skees, founder of The Designer's Creative Studio, is a former Walt Disney Imagineering creative executive with over 30 years of experience leading cross-functional teams in the themed entertainment industry for large-scale global projects. He is an international speaker, has presented for The Disney Institute, lectured for multiple organizations and universities, and is a workshop facilitator. He has guided a variety of companies, from pharmaceuticals and design firms to e-commerce and retail, in the art of story-based brand experience creation. Theron is a founding member of The World Experience Organization (WXO) and sits on several advisory boards.

More by James Warda

Where Are We Going So Fast?: Finding the Sacred in Everyday Moments (Rowman & Littlefield, 2001)

A note on the type

The primary typefaces are mid-century in origin and design, befitting a work that celebrates the realization of Walt's dream in Anaheim. The main body is a flavor of Clarendon, inspired from the classic 1953 version by Hoffman and Eidenbenz that in itself was an adaptation of the original from the mid-nineteenth century. Quotes and Theron's Keys are set in Futura, developed by Paul Renner in 1927. Inspired by the simple, modern, and functional Bauhaus design conceits, Futura became highly favored throughout the mid-twentieth century (and beyond), utilized in advertising, industrial design, and even on the Apollo 11 plaque NASA left on the moon.

About Rivershore Press

Rivershore Press publishes seriously fun books on design, parks, and audio engineering. Find out more at www.rivershorepress.com.

Please take a moment and review this book wherever you bought it. It does help quite a bit, so thank you very much!

www.ingramcontent.com/pod-product-compliance
Lightning Source LLC
Chambersburg PA
CBHW070054030426
42335CB00016B/1890